Low a

Memories of a Cold War Fighter Pilot

Charles Banks

F-4E

F-105G

F-111E

ISBN 978-1-952311-08-6   (Color Paperback)
ISBN 978-1-952311-07-9   (B&W Paperback)
ISBN 978-1-952311-06-2   (eBook)

Published by Taxiway Publishing
Oak Hill, VA

<u>Dedication</u>

I dedicate this book to my family.

My wife, Barbara, who spent 17 of my 20 years in the Air Force as a fellow Air Force officer, moved with me to various locations as the Air Force directed, and served an additional 10 years in the Air Force Reserve after I retired.

This dedication is also to our two daughters.
Gwendolyn was born at George Air Force Base, California.
Dawn was born at RAF Lakenheath, England.

Gwen and Dawn strongly encouraged me to write all these stories. I agreed as a way to be sure that I didn't forget the stories in my later years. I have always tried hard to keep all stories to the exact truth without embellishment. This book will assure that they stay that way. However, it is possible that my memory of events over 40 years ago might not be perfect.

I also dedicate it to the thousands of men and women of the United States Military Services who gave all they had to defend our free country. May they all be remembered for their love of country, willingness to serve, and bravery when faced with the perils of national defense.

Close Call, but an Air Medal

One night in September '72, I was number 2 in an F-4D 2-ship Close Air Support mission. We were trying to help a surrounded South Vietnamese Army (SVN) unit that got into a much larger engagement than expected near Quang Tri.

The Forward Air Controller (FAC), call sign Covey, was out of flares and his rockets wouldn't fire, so he couldn't show us where to drop. All we could see was a blank black area with sparkles of artillery explosions carpeting the place. The artillery fire was from both sides. We couldn't tell friendlies from bad guys since the friendlies were nearly surrounded.

We reached Bingo fuel and had to head back toward Korat Air Base, Thailand. A few minutes after we left, artillery started a fire in the middle of the main group of North Vietnamese troops, so the FAC asked us to come back.

We went back while the FAC arranged for us to land at Da Nang (the only base within our fuel range by then) instead of Korat. The FAC had us drop our 2 strings of 12 MK-82 bombs west to east with one string on each side of the fire. That would head us right for Da Nang and get us on the ground safely with our low fuel state.

Lead rolled in aiming left of the fire. I rolled in aiming right of the fire. I thumbed the pickle button and felt my 12 bombs depart their racks. Pulling off target after the 30 degree dive, I was blinded by huge explosions in my rear-view mirrors. As we turned right, I looked back and saw the largest explosions I have ever seen growing and spreading over a large area. "What the Hell was THAT?" yelled my Weapon System Officer from the back seat.

While pulling 5 Gs to avoid a twin line of red 23mm tracers from north of the target area, I grunted "Don't know, but it sure blew up!"

It turned out to be an ammunition dump that a battalion of North Vietnamese regulars was guarding. We found out later that the SVN unit we were supporting used the chaos to get away with all their guys. There was no way to estimate enemy casualties, but FACs reported that the place burned and exploded for 2 ½ days!

Unfortunately, on our way to Da Nang, a rocket attack hit and cratered both Da Nang runways, closing them. We asked Panama, the area radar controller, for a tanker over the water or over South

Vietnam. Bad news. None were around. The few places north or west of Da Nang where an F-4 could land were closed months previously. All we could do was head for Nankon Phenon AB (NKP) in Thailand, the closest place we could land.

That was also where the Search and Rescue (SAR) forces were based. We hoped we could at least make it into Thailand. We jettisoned our empty drop tanks to reduce weight and drag and climbed to about 45,000 feet to get as much range as possible.

After many calculations and recalculations, we realized that Lead couldn't make it across Laos to Thailand, and I could probably just make the Thai border, but not to NKP. The GCI controller started to arrange a SAR, and we developed a plan for Lead to glide as far as possible and eject at 5,000 feet. I would follow him down, circle once to record their location, then see how far west I could get before doing the same thing.

Of course, it was about 2 AM, so the location wasn't going to be very accurate. We had no idea what terrain we would end up in. It could be jagged karst mountains, jungle, or flat plain. We did all we could do to prepare for ejection if our engines went silent.

As Lead's fuel gauge approached zero and I had maybe 5 minutes left, a tanker called on Guard frequency. He said they heard of our situation and had the throttles to the wall "heading across the fence" (That's the Thailand/Laos border.) We had never heard of a tanker flying into Laos before.

We pulled the throttles to idle and coasted down to his 24,000' altitude using very little fuel. He did the most perfect "tanker turn onto fighter" maneuver that I have ever seen and rolled out of his left 180 degree turn less than 100 feet in front of us just as we leveled at his altitude. Kudos to the tanker crew and Lead WSO!

The Boomer plugged into Lead with the boom fully extended and pumped a few hundred pounds in. I stayed tucked tight on Lead's right wing. I no longer bothered looking at my fuel gauge, because it had stopped at the bottom. Then, I connected, got some fuel, and we all started breathing again. We both took plenty of fuel to get back to Korat and even divert if necessary.

The next day, we wrote up the paperwork to nominate the KC-135 crew for a Distinguished Flying Cross (DFC). I don't know what became of that. They certainly deserved it. They saved two F-4s for sure and likely the four of us. No one who bailed out in that area of Laos returned unless they were rescued within a few hours. We were also nominated for a DFC, but it was downgraded to a single-mission Air Medal.

Each mission into North Vietnam was worth 2 points. SVN, Laos, and Cambodia were worth 1 point. 20 points was worth an Air Medal. Air Medals could also be awarded for single missions.

We arranged for the tanker crew to be well supplied with drinks at the Utapao AB Officer's Club. I think it was a case of Chivas Regal Scotch.

On the way to Korat AB, I got to thinking, "How did I get from the nice classrooms at Purdue to be in this situation strapped into the ejection seat of a deadly fighter over hostile territory at age 25?"

Contents

Chronology

- Jun 1965, Graduated from Valparaiso High School, Valparaiso, Indiana
- Aug 1965-Jun 1970, Purdue University, at Lafayette, Indiana
- Jun 5, 1970, Graduated from Purdue University, BS in Technology Management
- Jun 6, 1970, Commissioned into United States Air Force as Second Lieutenant (2Lt)
- Jun 9, 1970, Reported to Laredo Air Force Base (AFB), Texas for Undergraduate Pilot Training (UPT)
- Jun 9, 1970-Jul 2, 1971, T-41, T-37, T-38 at Laredo Air Force Base, Texas
- Aug 1971-Jan 1972, F-4C training at George AFB, California
- Jan 1972, Water Survival at Homestead AFB, Florida
- Mar 1972-Apr 1972, F-4D training at Kunsan Air Base, Korea
- May 1972-Oct 1972, F-4D and F-4E at Korat Air Base, Thailand, flying combat in Vietnam
- Oct 1972-Apr 1973, F-4D at Kunsan Air Base, Korea
- Apr 1973-May 1973, O-2 training at Hurlburt Field, Florida
- May 1973-Jun 1975, O-2A at Bergstrom AFB, Austin, Texas
- Jul 1975, 2-week T-38 Jet Recurrency training at Holloman AFB, New Mexico
- Jul 1975-Nov 1975, F-105D & F transition training at McConnell AFB, Kansas
- Nov 1975-Jul 1979, F-105G at George AFB, CA
- Aug 1979-Sep 1980, Civilian Engineer with Grumman Aircraft Corporation at NAS Point Mugu, CA
- Oct 1980-Jan 1981, F-111D training at Canon AFB, New Mexico
- Feb 1981-Feb 1984, F-111F at Royal Air Force (RAF) Lakenheath, England
- Mar 1984- Mar 1987, Air Liaison Officer for 2nd Brigade, 2nd Armored Division, Fort Hood, TX
- Mar 1987-Feb 1989, Fighter Liaison Officer for 2nd Armored Division, Fort Hood, TX
- Feb 1989-Feb 1992, Joint Firepower Control Course Manager, Hurlburt Field, FL
- Feb 29, 1992, Retired from Active Duty

Prologue

In 1972, what we called fighter aircraft were just that, aircraft that were directly involved in the fight against enemy aircraft, air defenses, and ground forces. Clearly, some efforts were underway to figure out how to make an aircraft "stealthy", but those of us flying then hadn't been told. The term "Stealth" was used in talks about Submarines and Special Operations for sneaking around. How could a huge hunk of reflective metal blasting along with a deafening roar trailing a blue flame possibly be stealthy? Maybe someday.....

Our idea for getting through enemy defenses was low and fast. A defense contractor study determined that the chance of making it through projected defenses was over 90% if the aircraft flew at 100 feet and above Mach 1.2. The question to be answered was, "Where would we train if the sonic boom from flying at that speed and altitude destroyed everything in its path?"

Most of the Century Series fighters (F-100, 101, 102, 104, 105 and 106), built during the 1950's and 60's were designed to function primarily as air-to-air fighters with precision bombing as a secondary mission. The F-105 was the only one designed primarily as a bomber, and included an internal bomb bay. They depended on high speed and very low flying to penetrate defenses. They were all single-engine and single-seat except for a few training versions with a second seat.

The next generation included the F-4 (The prototype was called F-110.) and the F-111. These added a second engine and a Weapons System Operator in a second cockpit seat. The F-4 quickly took over most missions from the Century Series aircraft early in the Vietnam War. The F-105 continued for a few more years in the unique role of defense suppression as the F-105G. The F-106 continued air defense of the US until 1988.

This is a story about combat flying during those days and preparing for even bigger wars.

Please forgive me for using the term "guys" often. The Air Force assigned the first woman to a fighter in 1993, the year after I retired.

My Path to an Air Force Career

Born August 27, 1947, two years after WWII ended, I grew up in a world where aviation was a very rapidly growing field. I heard many stories from relatives and friends who fought in the war serving in the Army or Navy with many stories about their adventures. I heard little about the Air Force except that life in the Air Force was a lot better. My world at that time revolved in and around Valparaiso, Indiana, where my father, Lloyd Hubert Dunn, and my mother, Zelma Lucile (Phillips) Dunn, grew up.

War

My father and my grandfather, Gordie Phillips, were working at US Steel in Gary, Indiana, when WWII started. They tried to volunteer for a Service, but steel workers were needed to make more steel than ever before. As a result, they were turned down and told to expect a lot of new steel workers to train.

A few years later, the Korean War increased the visibility of air combat as we all saw news reels before each movie in the local theaters. I was still too young to understand what a war meant, but I knew my mother and a couple of her friends worked at a plant in Whirlpool, Indiana, making artillery shells.

The horror caused by war sometimes reached the home front. One day, my mother's friend was working on the quickly moving line for making 105mm shell casings. She accidentally drilled a half-inch hole through the palm of her hand instead of the shell case. That was very traumatic to all at the plant and at our homes.

Further trauma for my sister, Marlene, and I was the divorce of our parents during the Korean War. My father left the area, moving to California. My mother remarried two years later, and we were adopted by our stepfather, Joseph Thomas Banks.

Joe Banks had been in the Navy during WWII. His first enemy encounter resulted in a Japanese shell hitting his 5-inch gun turret on his destroyer. He was the only survivor in the turret. He spent the rest of the war as a cook's assistant. During the Korean War, he went to work at US Steel with my grandfather.

The worst thing my stepfather witnessed during the Korean War was a young, new steelworker falling into the vat of molten steel in an open hearth furnace. He and my grandfather continued making vast quantities of steel.

Peace and Cold War

After the war, life settled down to a new normal. Everyone was happy, and becoming more prosperous. I attended the just completed Northview Elementary School less than two blocks from our house for six years. I even had a new brother, Gary Ray Banks.

During that time, tensions were growing with Russia, and the "Cold War" began. A Nike Antiaircraft Missile site was built just north of town as part of the ring to protect Chicago, Illinois. At school, we were all taught to "duck and cover" if we saw the flash of an atomic bomb. The windows of my classroom faced toward Chicago, which was about 50 miles away. Most of that distance was across Lake Michigan. About half way along the coast to Chicago were Whiting and East Chicago, Indiana. A large part of those cities was oil refineries and steel mills along the shore of Lake Michigan.

On my birthday, August 27, 1955, a Saturday, I was at the school for practice for some special event that I don't remember, since it never happened. My third grade class had gathered in a classroom for the teachers to tell us all about it. While we were sitting in our seats, the entire sky toward Chicago lit up in a gigantic fireball! About two minutes later was the sound of an unbelievably huge explosion. The windows bulged in and out like they were going to blow in. There was no doubt at all in any teacher or student's mind that Chicago had just been nuked!!!

Several more explosions were heard over the next hour as we all cowered under our desks, expecting to die at any second. Some screamed. Some cried. Some were just paralyzed. I kept thinking about what to do if we survived.

Finally, maybe two hours later, we got word that the Standard Oil Refinery in Whiting had exploded. Here a link to the Whiting Refinery Fire in 1955.

https://www.pophistorydig.com/topics/whiting-refinery-fire-1955/

A year later, I went through a similar, but smaller event when a bulldozer about two miles out from my classroom hit a gas line. The gas line exploded, throwing the bulldozer over thirty feet into the air, killing the operator.

We again executed the "duck and cover" routine. This time, there wasn't a flash, but the sound was shocking.

2

During those days, awaiting the Russian missiles that never came was scary, especially for children, and news was limited to the 6pm and 11pm broadcasts. Most of my friends and I developed a strong sense of duty to defend the United States. A few thought that just loving our enemies would bring peace. I wanted to be able to fight back, not just cower under a desk.

Auto Racing

Life at home went on as usual. Every Sunday evening my entire family went to the stock car races at Rensselaer, Indiana, a one hour drive south of Valparaiso. It was a quarter-mile oval dirt track. The races were always very competitive and exciting.

A good friend and neighbor of ours, Dave Whitcomb, had a car and raced there. Dave was one of the best drivers and often won. He lived only a block from us, and my stepfather and I helped work on his car during the week. I learned a lot about racing from Dave. I wanted to race as soon as I could drive.

One Sunday, I learned that the dangers in racing are not just on the track. A tire came off of a car at top speed on the back straight of the oval track. Straight off the end of that straightaway was the pits. The tire hit another car, flew high into the air, over the fence, and landed in the pits. Unfortunately, the guy standing talking to my Dad in the pits turned to look when someone yelled. The tire hit him square in the face and smashed his head between it and the fender of a car, killing him instantly. I learned that safety must be a priority around dangerous equipment. Also, keep checking six. That's aviation speak for the 6 o'clock position, directly behind you. If the enemy is there, you're in big trouble. It is very hard to shoot an enemy fighter with the gun from anywhere other than straight behind it.

I entered the Soapbox Derby every year I was eligible, age 12 to 16. I strictly followed the rules and built the car myself, working in my grandfather's garage where he taught me how to use all the tools. I learned that exact alignment of the axles combined with a smooth, accurate steering system were the most important factors for acceleration in those gravity-powered cars.

Most Soapbox Derby car builders spent most of their time building the car sleek and low for optimum aerodynamics to minimize wind drag. However, the cars start from a standstill and slowly accelerate to a top speed of about 35 miles per hour. Wind drag is negligible at those speeds. The slight drag caused by turning a wheel to steer is far more important.

I almost won the local race when I was 16. After all the elimination heats, I was in the final heat which was -the best 2 out of 3 set of races. I had three dead heats before a photo finish showed the other guy wining by an eighth of an inch. I was edged out of the win by a guy who then won the national event at Akron, Ohio, and the 4-year college scholarship it comes with. No one came within a car-length of him. I lost that scholarship by an eighth of an inch in the photo finish. I got a 4-inch trophy for second place and learned a great lesson that speed and timing was everything.

I was 14 when my grandfather bought a go kart for me. I drove it around in the county fairground behind his house. The next year, I started racing each week at a dirt track outside of town.

My first day of racing was a huge ego-boost. I was second fastest qualifier. The first race at each event was the trophy dash. That was the first and shortest race of the day and consisted of the six fastest qualifiers racing for six laps. I *won*! I still have that trophy, the first of many racing trophies.

During the last race of the season, I was passing the leader in the feature race when he slid out into my side. My left rear tire ran over his tire, sending me end-over-end six times. I spent the off season rebuilding my kart and repainting my crash helmet.

I never missed watching the Indy 500 on Memorial Day or listening to it on the radio. I attended it twice and attended qualifying several times. I also attended many other races at Indianapolis Raceway Park," Illiana Speedway" on the Indiana/Illinois state line, and Soldier Field in Chicago. Since I lived near the US-30 Dragstrip, I got to see many famous drag racers and even the first jet powered racers including Walt Arfons Green Monster.

Aviation

Aviation entered my life later and slower than racing. I was first inspired when I was in elementary school. My maternal grandfather lived one block from us. His house backed up to the county fairground where there were numerous large elm and oak trees. Living in those trees were several families of flying squirrels.

I could sit in the back yard for hours watching those squirrels glide from tree to tree. It looked so effortless. Other squirrels had to expend energy to run down a tree, run to another, and run up it. I was jealous of those flying squirrels.

There was an airport close to the house where I lived, so I saw planes every day. There was even an annual air show. I never missed one. I found precision flying amazing and wondered what it was like to do that. What did it feel like? Was it frightening? How long did it take to learn those maneuvers? How do you become a pilot?

I witnessed one accident during an air show at our airport. A Stearman biplane was doing an aerobatic show. Just a few seconds before he would have landed, he did an outside snap roll. Pieces flew off, the left wings folded up against the fuselage, and it went straight down, crashed, and burned.

The investigation showed that the crankshaft had broken. Half of the prop hit the pilot in the chest, killing him instantly. The other half flew to the left and cut wires and struts supporting the left wings. That was traumatic for all spectators. I can still see every second of it.

I started building and flying model airplanes including powered planes controlled by wires. These were called "U-Control" planes. You would stand and fly the plane in circles around yourself controlling the elevator for up and down with a hand-held controller with wires running to the plane.

When I was a teenager, the first movie that was not a cartoon or comedy that I saw was "Flying Tigers." What heroes! My model building became all fighters. I even had a U-Control F-4U Corsair. Later, I saw two movies about Strategic Air Command, "Bombers B-52" and "A Gathering of Eagles." Welllllll, I kept building fighters.

I became a science fiction fan early and especially enjoyed space movies and books. I never missed an episode of the original Star Trek. There were no video recorders at that time. I was almost 14 when President John F. Kennedy made his historic speech declaring the moon landing program. It was clear that space travel including a huge orbiting Space Station, a Moon Base, and a Mars Base would become routine during my lifetime. I'm still waiting for some of that.

I soon decided that I wanted to be an astronaut. As I read about the backgrounds of the early astronauts, it appeared that the way to get there was to be a good fighter pilot. It was even better if you could also become a test pilot.

Beyond five years old, I had no exposure to family with education greater than tenth grade, so I didn't understand what a higher education provided. I thought that college was something rich kids did

5

to become businessmen, lawyers, or doctors. I found out that becoming a military pilot or astronaut required a degree, so I started considering college.

My grandfather told me I should be an engineer, because I thought like one. Not knowing anything about engineering, I dismissed the idea, wondering why he thought I should drive trains.

My senior year, thanks to my excellent Valparaiso High School college prep curriculum, I cleared up this misunderstanding and started thinking about getting an engineering degree.

I started looking at what college I wanted to attend. As an Indiana resident, I looked primarily at Indiana schools. My family couldn't possibly afford an out-of-state school. Notre Dame sent me an offer, but they didn't have a degree option that I wanted.

Purdue University

June 1965

Before I graduated from high school, I decided to go to Purdue University to pursue an Aeronautical Engineering degree. The decision for Purdue was a combination of its reputation as an outstanding Aeronautical Engineering program and that it was a state school with tuition of only $165 per semester. That was helped when the Purdue Alumni Association gave me a $100 per semester scholarship.

Due to Purdue being formed as a Land Grant College, the law required all men to take Reserve Officer Training Corps (ROTC) for the first two years. It could be any of the four services. You could drop ROTC after two years.

If you chose to continue after two years, you would receive a stipend of $50 per month during your junior and senior years with an agreement that you would be commissioned an officer at graduation and enter your Service for at least four years. I planned to work part time to pay for being at Purdue, so the stipend was attractive. Of course, I chose Air Force ROTC.

That summer, Congress passed a law terminating the ROTC requirement. I received a letter from Purdue telling me that I could drop my scheduled one-credit Air Force Military Science course and replace it with something else. I decided to take the ROTC course and

6

get an easy "A" in something that interested me. ***That decision set the course for the rest of my life!***

I tested out of most Freshman courses and ended up taking double-credit courses freshman year. To pay for room and board, I worked 30-hour weeks through most of college, so I took a light course load after Freshman year. After two years, I signed the agreement to enter the Air Force and get the stipend. Then, I changed majors twice, requiring a fifth year to get the last of the credits I needed. AF ROTC allowed me to take the fourth year off and return for my fifth year.

During my fourth year, it was time to take the Air Force Officer Qualification Test (AFOQT). I took the pilot test and scored 99th percentile. *I'm In*!

Later that year, we had the military physical exam.

Disaster! My eyes were 20/30. Pilot qualification required 20/20. Instead of getting the "1P" pilot code, I was given "1N" for navigator. I was given the option of dropping ROTC, but I figured at least I would be flying, so I stayed in.

During senior year, we were given a mini-physical to update records. This time, I tested 20/20!

Ecstasy! I was changed to "1P" and got an assignment to Undergraduate Pilot Training (UPT). I can't remember ever being happier up to that time.

At this time, I had to make another decision that would affect the rest of my life. I had been racing go-karts and running my car in autocrosses for several years. I did quite well, and it didn't go unnoticed.

Purdue Grand Prix

Purdue has an annual go-kart race a week before the Indy 500 called the Purdue Grand Prix. It is a long race taking a couple of hours. It was laid out as a half-mile road course in the stadium parking lot. By my Junior year, an actual track had been built.

The karts were require to have a roll bar and bumpers added on all sides. They were powered by a single, one-cylinder engine and were capable of over 50 mph.

The race rules required at least two pit stops for gas. My Freshman year, I participated with the team at my residence hall, Tarkington Hall. I was the only member of the team with significant racing experience. The policy was to use two or three drivers to allow more people to participate, so we planned driver changes during the pit stops.

One of the Tarkington team members was Ken Gleason. We were roommates our Sophomore year and both worked on the kart. While we were still in school, I was an usher at his wedding to Connie, his partner for life. We still keep in touch and visit each other when possible.

The Tarkington team settled on two drivers with two pit stops. I would drive the first third and last third of the race. I also drove the qualification laps and was fastest qualifier. That was on a kart one inch from the ground; *Low and Fast*.

When the race started with us at pole position, I pulled away and passed the entire field twice. At the first pit stop, we had a two-lap lead. The other driver had a few problems and lost the two laps and the lead. When I took over again, we were third place but close to second. I again passed the entire field until getting a full lap lead.

Several laps from the end of the race, I entered a very fast, sweeping, right turn. I saw a kart that had spun sitting backwards in the center of the track halfway around the turn. I hugged the inside of the turn to go by him.

Unfortunately, he made the bad decision to drive off the inside of the track just as I got there. We hit almost directly head-on. The impact tore my front bumper off and my left side bumper was dragging the track. It also bent my brake pedal and sprained my left ankle.

I kept going, but was given the black flag due to the bumpers. That was a real letdown for the entire team that had worked for months to get ready. It's hard to take a loss in a once-per-year event to a mistake made by someone else. Well, that's racing.

I raced one more Purdue Grand Prix. That time, I qualified second fastest. On race day, it had rained during the night. The race was started, but run under a yellow flag (no passing) for the first five laps to dry the track. I got the lead quickly, because the pole position kart spun off the track on the first turn of the first lap. I led the first 17 laps, but the engine seized on lap 18.

I started working 30-hours per week, and didn't have time to participate again.

We got permission from Purdue to take the kart to Greenfield, IN, just east of Indianapolis to participate in a national championship points race. It was one of about a dozen races each year to determine a national champion, but it would be the only one we would run due to the locations spread all over the country. Of course, we removed the roll bar and bumpers to bring it to standards and installed a larger fuel tank. With the lighter weight and different gearing, the kart was able to reach 70 mph on the main straightaway. Still low and even faster.

There were about 40 karts that started the race. The track was about three fourths of a mile laid out in the streets and parking areas of a city park. It was a timed one-hour race with starting positions determined by a drawing. I started at sixteenth position.

After the start, I started catching and passing karts one by one. We didn't have pit signs or radios, so I had no idea how much time had passed or what position I was in. I finally caught up with the current national champion. After several attempts to pass him, I finally got by as we entered the main straightaway. I didn't know that I was now in second place! Also, the hour expired during that lap, making the next lap the last. Half way around that last lap, on a long straightaway, my engine seized. That locked the rear wheels. The national champ was still right behind me and couldn't dodge my suddenly slowing kart. He hit the rear of my kart, but was able to keep going. I had come within half a lap of finishing second in a national championship race.

Career Choices

A guy (whose name I can't remember) was putting together a United States Auto Club (USAC) stock car team with two cars and drivers. He contacted me, and we had a good conversation. He watched me win an autocross on the 2 ½ mile road course at Indianapolis Raceway Park.

About the same time that I had to make a final decision to go active Air Force or Air Force Reserves, I found out that the guy was going to make me an offer. To compound the difficulty of the decision, he was planning to start an Indy Car team in two years. He would move the stock car drivers up to Indy Cars and hire two more stock car drivers.

My two childhood dreams were suddenly competing for me! I decided that I could be an active duty pilot and find some time to race for fun. Of course, I would also have auto racing as a backup if I washed out of pilot training – not that I ever considered that possible. I think I made the right decision. *The "course" for my adult life became a "flight plan."*

Of course, the fact that I never heard of the guy again and can't remember his name probably means that he either never got the team going or it didn't do very well. Since I follow racing news, I would have heard of him. Maybe he would have done okay if I was driving for him, but I'll never know.

First Flight

Schweizer2-32-02

Prior to Undergraduate Pilot Training (UPT), I was only in an aircraft four times. The first was a backseat ride in a Schweitzer glider while at Purdue. Loved it! The tow plane towed us to about 3,000 feet. After the loud bang of releasing the tow hook, all was quiet. The pilot flew me to some nearby hills, then around the airfield a couple of times before landing. Soaring in near silence over the familiar farm fields of Indiana was a beautiful experience. The only sound was the whispering of airflow, giving the pilot subtle hints for control adjustments. Now, I was more excited than ever to make it into pilot training.

C-47

For my second flight, while an ROTC Cadet at Purdue, I was a passenger in an Air Force C-47 from Purdue to Wright-Patterson AFB, Ohio. Our AF ROTC instructors were the pilots. This is a very noisy ride. I was surprised at the steep slope of the floor while on the ground.

Amazingly, this was the comfort level that many early airline passengers experienced.

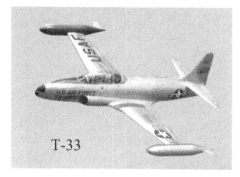
T-33

The third flight was a 20-minute ride in the back seat of a T-33 while at Wright-Patterson AFB. We did some very mild aerobatics. Yes, I got sick, just like almost all the cadets. Unfortunately, all I had to puke into was my glove. Yuk. That is the only time I was ever air sick. The fourth flight was an uneventful C-47 trip back to Purdue.

XB-70

The trip included a great tour of the Air Force Museum. We even got to visit the only remaining XB-70. It had just been flown there to go into the museum. It was parked on an outlying ramp having all fuel and other volatiles dried out before going on permanent display. Our guide pointed out that the XB-70 is longer than the Wright Brothers' first flight.

XB-70
Valkyrie

I never became an astronaut, but some of my classmates at Purdue did. Purdue has more astronaut graduates than any other civilian school.

Laredo Air Force Base, TX

https://en.wikipedia.org/wiki/Laredo_Air_Force_Base
June 1970

Arrival Crashes #1 & #2

This wasn't a crash, but it was serious. Just before I arrived at Laredo, a T-37 in the traffic pattern at Hirsch Field, the Laredo auxiliary field, hit a turkey buzzard. It came through the right side of the canopy, hitting the instructor pilot in the face, breaking his neck, and killing him.

Another T-37 was in the Hirsch pattern so the instructor in that plane took control and joined up with the stricken plane. The wind noise through the broken windscreen made radio talk impossible, so all he could do was use hand signals. The pre-solo student followed standard procedures that he had just learned and landed the T-37 without serious problems. He was presented an Air Medal at his class graduation ceremony.

Also, that week, a check pilot and a crew chief took a T-37 up for a Functional Check Flight. That's a test flight done after any maintenance on vital systems such as flight controls or engines. The last part of the test is to put it into a spin for three turns, then recover.

This is a maneuver that all students are required to do several times. It teaches you how to handle an out-of-control situation. Recovery in the T-37 is done by applying full rudder the opposite direction of the spin and slamming the stick full forward for a moment. This results in a steep dive, gaining speed, and back to fully under control.

However, their sticks wouldn't move more than halfway forward. They both pushed as hard as they could, even bending the sticks. Unable to recover, they ejected at about 5,000 feet. The plane continued spinning to impact, leaving the exact burned outline of a T-37 with all parts about where they belong. The investigators found a screwdriver jammed in the stick mechanism below the floor.

All Air Force aircraft maintainers' toolboxes have stiff foam with cutout spots for every tool. A check of that crew chief's toolbox found that it was missing that screwdriver. He must have left it inside the plane and it rolled into that spot during the spin. The check pilot was unhurt, but the crew chief landed on the only barbed wire fence within miles and received severe cuts.

Welcome to pilot training, Chuck!

Undergraduate Pilot Training (UPT)

UPT at that time was a one-year program using the T-41A, T-37, and T-38. Total flight hours were about 200. Physical fitness was an important part of the training with sports events of various types and a lot of mile-and-a-half runs. I was in class 72-01. The number was because it was the first class scheduled to graduate in fiscal year 1972. In those days, the fiscal years started in July, so we graduated the first week of July of 1971.

Bowling

I was a big bowler during this time. At Purdue, I was the number six man on the Purdue bowling team. That means that I was first alternate for the 5-man team. I was never needed for a tournament, but I could practice for free all I wanted. When I got to Laredo, it was about time for annual leagues to start, so I checked for openings at a bowling alley right off the end of the Laredo runways.

A guy had just quit, leaving one team with only four bowlers. They asked me what I would average. I didn't want them to think I was exaggerating, so I said, "Probably 175 or 180." They jumped at that and said I would be the best bowler on the team.

We started league play that night. I had just driven all day from Indiana and was tired. Of course, I wasn't familiar with the lanes, either. Through the first game, I struggled. I couldn't pick up spares. I rolled a 104! I hadn't been that low since junior high school.

By the end of the game, the guys were sitting away from me, not talking, and looking angry. They thought I had lied about my average. Well, I did, but not the way they thought. I finished that first game with a strike and spare.

When the second game started, I rolled a strike, then another, and another, and another. I only missed a strike twice. I ended up with 256. Suddenly, I was welcome again. I finished that league with a 192 average, had the highest average and single game on the team, and we took second place for the season.

Academics

The first few weeks of UPT were intensive academics on everything a pilot needs to know. This continued for the entire year with concentrated sections on the systems and procedures of each type of aircraft before flying it.

A theme that entered the training very early was, "Speed is Life." Aircraft fly due to air flow over and under the wings. The faster you go, the more lift you create. It is essential to always be going fast enough to create the lift needed. Thus, "Speed is Life."

Also, when in combat, the faster you go, the harder you are to hit. When you are the target, speed reduces the reaction time available to air defenses. "Speed is Life."

Special concentration was on emergency procedures. The most critical emergency procedures are printed in boldface type in the checklist. Those must be memorized so that they can be accomplished immediately with no reference to the checklist.

We were tested on those constantly. They were even taped to the inside of toilet stall doors. I never had an emergency during UPT, but over the next 20 years, I used several of those procedures on each type of aircraft.

During these first weeks, everyone received a very comprehensive physical exam. A few hopefuls failed the physicals. It also included basic survival training including a parasail flight towed by a pickup truck. That was fun, but they would only let you do in once.

Two of the guys in my class were black guys that turned out to have the sickle-cell anemia trait in their blood. That was thought to indicate that they would develop the anemia at some time. You can't tolerate high altitudes with that anemia. That disqualified them from flying and had kept many blacks out of UPT over the years.

About two years later, it was discovered that most with the trait never actually developed the anemia. At that time, all those who had been washed out for that reason were invited to change their careers and attend UPT.

T-41A Mescalero

https://en.wikipedia.org/wiki/Cessna_T-41_Mescalero
http://www.militaryfactory.com/aircraft/detail.asp?aircraft_id=172

The first aircraft I flew was the T-41 Mescalero. This was a two-week series of flights learning the basic techniques and rules of flying, Air Force (AF) procedures, and basic flying discipline. The final flight was the student's initial solo flight. (That's without the instructor in the plane.) For me, it all went well.

T-37 Tweet

https://en.wikipedia.org/wiki/Cessna_T-37_Tweet

The next trainer was the T-37 Tweet. The T-37 was known as the "Tweet" because of the ear-piercing screech made by the centrifugal-flow compressor section of the engines, which were of an early jet design. The T-37 was built by Cessna Aircraft. A later version of it

became the A-37. The A-37 had the much more powerful engines from the T-38 and could carry bombs, rockets, and guns. It was used extensively in Vietnam by both USAF and the South Vietnamese Air Force. Cessna later used the basic design of its internal systems for one of the first business jets, the Citation.

Ike Hirsch Auxiliary Airfield,

Laredo Auxiliary 2, call sign "Barfly", was used for traffic pattern and landing practice by Laredo T-37 students. On each flight, initial takeoff and final landing were at Laredo AFB. All trainees soloed the T-37 at Hirsch. It was in the traffic pattern at Hirsch that the T-37 struck a Turkey Buzzard that killed the instructor pilot.

The first jet solo flight was a big event. This was usually the sixth flight. After a few practice landings with the Instructor Pilot (IP), you would land, taxi to the ramp while shutting down the right engine, let the IP out, restart the right engine, takeoff, do two touch and go landings, do a full stop, taxi to the ramp and pick up the IP.

T-37

After arriving back to Laredo AFB and parking the T-37, the new pilot would be carried to a nearby small swimming pool and thrown in. July in Laredo was warm enough for this celebration. Normally, this would be on the 6th flight. Many who "washed out" of UPT never made it to T-37 solo.

I was nervous on my first T-37 solo. This was mostly because my instructor was one of those who never completely let go of the stick during instruction flights! I had never actually landed the aircraft on my own until I was solo, but I felt that I could do it okay. To my great relief, I got top scores on all three landings. This first jet solo is a huge step towards the competence and confidence needed to fly military aircraft. With my confidence established, I completed the T-37 program in the minimum number of flights. I also excelled in academics during that time.

T-38 Talon

https://en.wikipedia.org/wiki/Northrop_T-38_Talon

The last 6 months of training were in the T-38 Talon. If someone measured everything about me; size, reaction time, thinking speed,

whatever; and designed an aircraft specifically for me, it would be identical to the T-38. I could fly it well from the first flight.

The T-38 is the sports car of the Air Force. It couldn't do anything but fly, and it did that extremely well. In later years, they added a bomb sight and racks for practice bombs for training pilots heading for fighters. More recently, they updated the 1950's era cockpit instruments with modern digital systems.

Of all the aircraft that I flew in the Air Force, the T-38 is the only one still in use. The first one was built in 1959. I once flew one that had only 18 hours on it. An average training flight was 1.2 hours. There was a 60th anniversary celebration for the first T-38 flight in April 2019.

I was well above average in the T-37 and tied with a few others for perfect scores in academics, but the T-38 made my career as a fighter pilot possible.

The thrill of lighting those two afterburners for your first T-38 takeoff can't be described. The acceleration is amazing. The takeoff takes only a few seconds during which you have to steer down centerline using your feet on the rudder pedals, check engine instruments and acceleration to assure proper operation, keep track of your speed, and rotate the nose up ten degrees at 135 knots to takeoff at 160 knots. In those few seconds, you accelerate to nearly three times the highway cruising speed of a normal car. I can't describe flying the

T-38 better than this article by Major Buck Wyndham, http://www.warbirdalley.com/articles/t38pr.htm.

Extra flights

I advanced to the final check ride in each segment of T-38 flight training early, since I could perform all required maneuvers proficiently. This provided an unexpected bonus. As we neared the end of UPT, I had finished all check rides two weeks early. At the same time, we were short of IPs. Those flights near the end require 4-ship formations. Normally, aircraft 1 and 3 (element leads), would be flown by students with IPs in the back seat, and students would fly solo in 2 and 4.

Several days during the last week, I was asked to fly solo as number 3 to complete a 4-ship. This was quite an honor, since flying as 3 required good leader techniques not usually trusted to students. The most challenging was 4-ship close trail formation aerobatics. Each aircraft flies just below and behind the one ahead of it. During barrel rolls, loops, and some other aerobatic maneuvers, it's very difficult for 3 and 4 to perform these maneuvers, requiring 3 to fly a difficult position smoothly.

Yes, every pilot who graduates from Air Force UPT has flown many of the same formation maneuvers as the Thunderbirds, but a couple of feet farther apart and at much higher altitude where you can recover from a mistake.

Famous Instructor?

Every student is given a few flights with someone other than his regular IP. I arrived at the briefing room one morning, and the IP name by my name just said "Visiting." I asked what that meant. The answer was "You're flying with an IP from the flight room next door."

I went down the hall to the next room and looked at the schedule board. It said that my IP was Doolittle. Okay, I know all about the famous Jimmy Doolittle of the 1930's. Who's pulling a joke on me?

I went to my regular IP and asked who I was to fly with.

He said, "Jimmy Doolittle."

I said, "He would be over 70. I don't think so."

My IP laughed and said, "Lieutenant Jimmy Doolittle 3rd, his grandson."

Attacked by a Dust Devil

The only real exciting event during pilot training (other than initial solo in each aircraft) was during an early solo flight in the T-38. I was doing touch-and-go landings at Laredo. I was about 30 feet above the end of the runway near touchdown when a huge dust devil (whirlwind filled with dust) came from my right directly into my path. It flipped me into 90 degrees of right bank instantly.

I simultaneously rolled upright, went to full afterburner (which the Air Force calls Max Power), and pulled the nose up quickly but gently due to the low airspeed. The deflection to the right caused me to be heading straight for the mobile control unit where there is always an instructor for safety and to grade each landing, as well as a student logging everything.

They dived out the door, thinking I was going to hit the unit. I pulled up as hard as I could at that low speed and passed about 20 feet over the top. Many students at that level of experience might pull too hard and get into an accelerated stall, resulting in the aircraft hitting the ground or mobile. The instructor got back into the mobile unit and complimented me on the radio for a "great save." Of course, the high roll rate and almost instantaneous max power the T-38 provides made the save possible.

Fini Flight

Traditionally, the last flight would be a single-ship solo with no specific training goals. Just have fun. That, of course, means lots or aerobatics. There were two of us essentially tied for top T-38 student (although that's not actually calculated). I was just going to have fun, but the other guy asked our flight commander if we could brief some 2-ship maneuvers and join up after takeoff. He agreed and scheduled our flights at about the same time.

There was no radar monitoring in our work areas and no altitude limits south of San Antonio in those days. I can't remember the other guy's name but, as per plan, he took off first and I joined up within a couple of minutes after arriving into our adjoining work areas. We flew all the standard aerobatic maneuvers as a 2-ship formation and swapped lead so we both did them as lead and wingman. At the planned time, he headed back for Laredo first.

During my 5-minute delay, I tried something I had always wanted to do. I knew that the engines work well even at high altitude and very low airspeed, so I took advantage of our huge, unlimited altitude work area. I did a shallow dive to 5,000 feet in full afterburner while accelerating to just under Mach 1, about 650 knots.

Then, I did a four-G pull into a vertical climb and shoved the stick full left. That put me into a vertical climb at Max power while rolling at nearly 2 rolls per second. I counted rolls, but lost count somewhere around 36 while concentrating on recovering without losing control.

At about 40,000 feet, I was rapidly losing airspeed. Remember, "Speed is Life." So I stopped the roll, eased the throttle back to a mid-setting, and used a lot of rudder to bring the nose down before losing too much speed to maintain control.

I topped out at about 45,000 feet and about 70 knots. It was similar to a very high Hammerhead Stall, a standard maneuver you see at air shows (but not by jets). Then, I headed back to Laredo for my final UPT landing.

Assignment Time

In those days, assignments were selected in a very simple manner. We started with 79 students, but only 56 graduated. The washouts went to non-pilot assignments, many to navigator training. Therefore, Class 72-01 at Laredo was given 56 pilot assignments.

The aircraft were listed on the right half of the chalk board, but no location was given. On the left, the graduating pilots were listed by class standing. I was seventh. Starting with number one, each student was asked which aircraft they wanted. As each student chose his aircraft, it would be crossed out.

Number one chose the only A-7; a single-seat, single engine, attack aircraft that the Navy used and the Air Force had just purchased. The first squadron was forming.

Number two took an RF-4, the reconnaissance version of the F-4. It takes photos and does not carry any weapons. Their motto was "Alone, Unarmed, and Unafraid."

Numbers three and four chose C-141's. At the time, this was the largest cargo aircraft in the Air Force. Both said they were going to spend the minimum six years in the Air Force and then go to airlines, so these assignments would give them large aircraft and large flight crew experience. Unfortunately, six years later, airlines were going bankrupt one after the other, and their pilots were being furloughed by the hundreds. I don't know how that worked out for any of them. They probably stayed in the AF.

Numbers five, six, and seven (me) took the three F-4's.

Number eight took the last fighter, an F-106.

Number nine took the second RF-4.

Eleven graduates selected KC-135's. Nine went to flight instructor training in T-37, T- 38, or T-41. The rest went to various transport aircraft including C-130's, C-141's, a C-9 medical airlift aircraft, and a T-39, the navigator trainer.

Two of the aircraft were a puzzle to us. They were QU-22B aircraft. Let's see. Our academic training told us "U" meant "Utility". However, "Q" meant unmanned drone! A little research showed that the AF had a few Beech Debonairs that had been converted into optionally piloted communication relay platforms.

They were being flown over Laos to relay data from sensors along the Ho Chi Minh Trail to sites in Thailand. The planes kept having minor problems that caused them to crash, but could be handled easily by a pilot. The decision was made to add a pilot who did nothing except takeoff and land unless he was needed to handle a problem. The rest of the flight would be six to eight hours orbiting over enemy territory, but not near air defenses, so these guys got a huge amount of "combat time!"

As was the case in each graduating class, the two B-52's went to the bottom two pilots. This is not to disparage the bottom of the class. *No one* graduates unless they pass the very rigid training requirements. The instructors must agree that all graduates are safe pilots and competent enough to fly their selected aircraft.

Several years later, Strategic Air Command forced a change to the assignment system, since they got all the bottom pilots. They wanted to get rid of this unfair stigma. I never saw the new process in action.

I was assigned to George AFB, CA, for the six-month F-4 training course. A few more months and I would finally be in a position to protect my country from the Russians and Chinese!

Departure Crash #1

Oh, yes. Laredo was the only one of seven pilot training bases that lost no aircraft during training missions during the year I was training, but just as I left, two instructors going to another base in a T-38 got into bad weather, couldn't get to a base to land soon enough, and ran out of fuel. They ejected from a perfectly good airplane after flaming out.

Little did I know, but a pattern had started.

Fate of Laredo AFB

Only two and a half years later, in Dec 1973, Laredo AFB was closed along with two other UPT bases due to a reduction in UPT after the Vietnam War ended. It was turned over to the city of Laredo, which used it as a Municipal Airport. In 1994, it was upgraded to become Laredo International Airport. Some of the old base is still in use including two of the three runways.

After Laredo closed, Hirsh Field was bought by a private party, and the runway was greatly expanded to a modern 10,000-foot runway with several buildings added. I don't know if that runway was ever used by aircraft, but it served as a Michelin tire test site for a few years. Hirsh is now abandoned.

George Air Force Base, California

https://en.wikipedia.org/wiki/George_Air_Force_Base

July 1971

This F-4C is the one flown by Col Robin Olds leading the famous mission where the new F-4Cs that had deployed to Ubon AB, Thailand, pretended to be F-105s loaded with bombs. In fact, they were F-4Cs loaded with air-to-air missiles. They fooled the NVN air force into attacking them, and eight MiG-21s were shot down. NVN only had 16 at the time. Col Olds got two of them with this F-4C, tail number 829.

In the late 1960's, the F-4Cs in Southeast Asia were replaced with F-4Es, which had a gun and performed far better against MiGs. This

23

aircraft was transferred to George AFB where I flew it three times during training.

Robin Olds Bio: https://en.wikipedia.org/wiki/Robin_Olds

Arrival Crash #3

The night before I arrived, a student pilot with an IP in the back seat flew that student's last training mission before graduation. It was a night bombing mission to Cuddeback Range. They had no idea that just at takeoff, the right main landing gear wheel broke off. No one on the ground saw it come off due to darkness. All indicators showed normal landing gear operation, because the sensors were on the strut, not the wheel.

When they lowered the landing gear to land, the Anti-Skid warning light came on. They followed normal procedure and turned the anti-skid off. Normally, you then just brake carefully so that you don't skid a tire. The flight was landing using night instrument procedures spaced about three miles apart, so no wingman was close to notice the missing wheel. The tower controller couldn't see it missing due to darkness.

When they landed, the strut put out a huge trail of sparks and gouged a grove into the runway. The student did a great job of maintaining control and keeping the aircraft on the runway during the thousand-foot slide. He got an Air Medal.

Unfortunately, as the strut ground down, the right external fuel tank dragged, wore through, and the residual fuel in it caught fire. After stopping and the crew evacuated, the fire got to the internal wing fuel tank, and the plane was burned too badly to repair. Welcome to F-4 training! Sounds a bit like arriving at Laredo!

F-4C Training

https://en.wikipedia.org/wiki/F-4C

The F-4 was flown by a pilot in the front cockpit and a Weapons System Operator (WSO), or an Instructor Pilot, in the rear cockpit. WSO's all complete Air Force Navigator School first. All three of the fighters that I flew were 2-seat except initial F-105 training was in the single-seat D version. I found that sharing the workload in high-speed combat is a great advantage over single seat.

The F-4 was typical of jet fighters at the time in that it had reliability problems. The saying went: "If there isn't a puddle of hydraulic fluid under it, then it doesn't have any in it." Nearly everything, including the radar, was manually controlled.

No one made it through the training without declaring an emergency for hydraulic, electrical, fuel system, or electronics failures. Of course, a major curriculum area was the training on how to handle all foreseeable emergencies. Simulator flights always included some simulated problems and a final one with cascading failures simulating combat damage and often ending with making the decision to eject and pull the ejection handle. That high-quality training saved many lives, including mine.

Basic F-4 training included academics for aircraft and weapons systems and flights for basic aircraft handling and aerobatics. The idea was to learn to fly the aircraft instinctively and get the maximum performance out of it.

Then, training moved into various types of 2-ship and 4-ship tactical formation flying. My extra 4-ship flights at Laredo turned to out to be a huge help. I again ended up flying positions usually flown by an instructor.

All that was learning to fly the aircraft. Training in how to actually use the aircraft for combat included high and low-level formation tactics, tactical navigation, and air-to-air refueling.

We learned several types of weapons deliveries including:
- Dive bombing at 10, 30, and 45 degrees;
- Level bombing at 50 and 100 feet (for napalm);
- Radar bombing;
- Toss bombing;
- 10 and 30 degree strafing with the 20mm gun pod (the F-4C and D did not have a built-in gun);
- 30 degree 2.75-inch rocket firing
- Air-to-air intercepts and air-to-air combat tactics including shooting the gun at the "dart", a 16-foot target being towed by another F-4.

Later, at Kunsan Air Base, I experienced the "fun" of flying the tow plane. There is no feeling like having several other planes shooting at a target you're towing just 1,500 feet behind.

The F-4 was a "Jack of all trades, Master of none" type of aircraft. It would do about any mission you could think of. Different pilots mastered different capabilities. My best was dive bombing.

I got through the six months of training with no problems. Well, few problems. I did have to declare an emergency for a rudder that kept going from side to side and another for a sagging aileron. Hey, it

25

was an old F-4C. There was also a weather divert to Naval Air Station China Lake for a surprise fog that formed all over Southern CA and Las Vegas.

Keep in mind that all the locations were in the Mojave Desert. Who expects fog in the desert?! We had a 4-ship flight doing dive bombing at Cuddeback Range. We were recalled due to worsening fog at George. Before getting back to base, George dropped below minimum visibility (1/4 mile), and we diverted to Nellis AFB at Las Vegas. When we were halfway there, Nellis dropped below minimums. We diverted again, this time to Naval Air Station China Lake with warnings that it was getting worse there, too.

We flew directly to the base and landed using visual approaches under a 300-foot ceiling with only a few minutes of fuel left. Larry and I had to land at the same time on runways that cross each other. We used braking and drag chute deployment timing to avoid getting to the intersection at the same time.

The weather folks were baffled at the freak sudden fog in the entire Mojave Desert. It formed in the Sierra Nevada Mountains and flowed into the desert.

The aileron problem appeared on my first check ride. It was a flight check for basic aircraft handling and included several standard aerobatic maneuvers. The IP in my back seat called out each maneuver he wanted to see, and I performed it.

When he called for a loop, I set up for a standard loop starting at 10,000 feet and 500 knots. I pulled up and went over the top at the right speed. Coming down the back side, as the G forces built up to 5G's, I found myself struggling to hold heading and finished 20 degrees left of the entry heading instead of on it. The IP said in a disappointed voice, "That wasn't so good, was it?"

He told me to try again. I had the same results. He then decided to show me how it was supposed to go. He ended up 25 degrees off heading.

Then, he said, "I'm adjusting the side mirrors to see the wings. Do it again." As I did the fourth loop, he said, "Ahah! I see the problem. When we pull G's, the left aileron is drooping two or three inches, causing drag on the left wing."

He passed me on all maneuvers. After landing, we reported the problem to maintenance. It turned out that the hydraulic aileron actuator was worn and couldn't hold the extra G force during the maneuver.

26

Windscreen Full of Desert

I only scared myself once during training. Over the middle of Death Valley, I was a wingman in a 2 vs 2 air combat mission when Lead reversed a diving turn twice. Trying to keep him in sight, I found myself pointed straight down at Mach 1.2 in full afterburner at 12,000 feet. I calculated later that it would have taken nine seconds to hit the ground.

Idle throttles, speed brakes out, and a 7-G pull got me out of it by 5,000 feet, which was much higher than I expected. Being over Death Valley helped provide plenty of altitude to recover. Of course, that was still good training.

I had a similar situation later while dodging an SA-2 over North Vietnam. That time, I left it in afterburner and only pulled 5 G's to maintain my speed. My training taught me the missile couldn't follow that maneuver. Sure enough, it couldn't.

Unexpected Training

My last training flight was in an F-4E. It wasn't planned that way, though. When we arrived on the flight line to our assigned tail numbers, mine was an E. I noticed that the IP had a C, so I walked over and pointed out that they seem to have given us the wrong tail numbers.

He said, "Do you think you can fly it?"

I said, "Well, I had the academics, and the checklist is in my helmet bag. Sure!"

So, he said, "Well, go ahead and take it."

So, my student WSO and I tore the plastic wrappers off the unused E checklists and hopped in. The weapons control panel and a few other things are very different. Also, it has slats instead of leading-edge flaps, and it has slots in the stabilator, making it much more sensitive in pitch at low speed, so I had to remember the different control techniques.

Takeoff technique is completely different, and you handle it very differently at high angle of attack. At high G loadings, all rolling is done with the rudder instead of the ailerons. Also, it lands 20 knots faster than the C. Later, at Korat AB, I was allowed to fly both the D and E models on combat missions due to this experience.

Even though I knew the control techniques and switch differences, I didn't appreciate how much more thrust the E engines had than the C.

We had briefed the standard light-weight eight-second spacing for starting our takeoff roll. This normally results in getting joined up with Lead at about 300 knots after 45 degrees or so turn. The E accelerated so fast that I caught lead and was in close formation before the landing gear and flaps were fully up.

The IP started a right turn and turned his head right to see how my join-up was going. He did a double-take when he saw me right on his wingtip!

After the flight, as we were walking back to the squadron building, he yelled, "What the Hell are you doing making a formation takeoff that wasn't briefed?

I pointed out that I actually used the briefed spacing, but the E caught up quickly.

He said, "Oh. I didn't think of that. We should increase the delay when a C is leading."

High and Fast

One flight during the latter part of aircraft maneuvering training was a Mach 2 run. The F-4 was capable of Mach 2 speed for a short time. All pilots need to know how to max perform the aircraft, so this flight is needed even though it is unlikely that Mach 2 would ever be reached in normal flying. To do this, you had to have a clean aircraft. That means no external stores including no external fuel tanks.

The F-4 is almost always flown with a drop tank under each wing and sometimes a larger tank on the centerline station under the fuselage. It cannot reach above Mach 1.6 with the drag of external stores. This flight would be with no external tanks and only internal fuel, about 14,000 pounds. The flight would be single ship with an IP in the back seat.

I filed a flight plan to use the Edwards AFB Mach 2 Corridor. That is an east to west route that passes over Edwards AFB and is aligned to avoid overflying towns. Many civilians don't like sonic booms.

Part of the flight planning was to check with the weather office to determine the coldest altitude below 50,000 feet. The F-4 is only certified to 50,000 feet. The coldest air will give the engines the most power. The high altitude is to reduce drag. An F-4 cannot even get supersonic near sea level. I think minimum temperature that day was at 47,000 feet.

I taxied onto the runway, held the brakes, pushed the engines up to 100% rpm, then checked the engine instruments to be sure everything was good. The brakes would hardly hold the screaming beast back.

Finally, I released the brakes and pushed the throttles to full afterburner at the same time. The acceleration without carrying the several thousand extra pounds we normally carried was exhilarating. We reached rotation speed very quickly.

Right after liftoff, I leveled at about 100 feet while retracting the landing gear and flaps. Staying level, we reached Mach 0.9 not far past the end of the runway. Then, I pulled into a climb, adjusting the climb angle to hold Mach 0.9. This gives the maximum rate of climb.

While climbing, a shallow left turn resulted in reaching the entry point for the Mach 2 Corridor shortly before reaching 47,000 feet. Leveling off then allowed the aircraft to accelerate to Mach 2.01. Each individual aircraft varies a little bit, so an F-4C will have a top speed of between Mach 1.95 and 2.05. Mach 2 is around 1,440 knots true airspeed. That's 1,657 Miles per Hour. That would go the 24 miles from Dulles Airport to Washington, DC, in just over a minute.

To demonstrate how poor pitch control is at that altitude and speed, the IP had me roll into 60 degrees of left bank and pull the stick full aft. That resulted in only 1 ½ Gs. During this, I didn't roll quite enough and accidentally climbed to 50,500 in just a couple of seconds. That is the highest I have ever been.

I was then to keep the stick full aft while rolling into a steeper bank to start a downward spiral. Now, he had me pull the throttles out of burner and slowly back to idle. Speed continued to decrease rapidly as G forces built up in the denser air. I eased the stick forward to hold 3 Gs until we slowed to about 300 knots and rolled out of the turn heading toward George AFB.

Still at idle throttle, I turned to line up with the runway about 3 miles out. When I got to a normal glide path, I brought the throttles up from idle and settled onto a normal approach speed about 125 knots.

The landing was only 20 minutes after takeoff and we had used nearly all our fuel.

Class Photo Tags

One thing that couldn't be ignored was the wall in the squadron snack bar. It had class photos of all the previous classes since the squadron became an F-4 training unit, about 12 or so. On each photo, they had plastic label tapes under each guy who was Killed In Action (KIA), Missing In Action (MIA), or confirmed to be a Prisoner of War (POW).

About half of the guys had stickers. Those who had been shot down and rescued or had an accident but weren't in one of those three categories did not have a label. It made you take your training very seriously. The best way to avoid getting a label is to be better than the enemy; that, plus a bit of luck.

In talking to guys in later years about all the accidents, I estimated that in the 1950-1975 time frame, about 60% of Air Force fighter pilots were involved in a major accident or combat shoot down. I met a pilot who ejected three times and an Electronic Warfare Officer (EWO) who survived two B-58 crashes, one on landing and one on takeoff. His pilot was killed in one of those.

Assignment Time

At the end of the F-4 class, assignments were handed out. Guys went to Europe, Alaska, Continental US, Philippines, Okinawa, Japan, Korea, Thailand, and Vietnam. Many of us ended up in Vietnam or Thailand at some time in the next couple of years.

I was assigned to the 8th Tactical Fighter Wing, Kunsan AB, Korea. (If the US owns the land, it's an Air Force Base. If another country owns the land, and we are a tenant, it's just an Air Base. In a United Kingdom country, it's a Royal Air Force Base.)

This was a bit of relief, because of the class photos. It was a relief to my family that I wasn't going to Vietnam. Of course, I felt like I wasn't pulling my load. I also felt that I could fly better than most of them, giving me a better chance of making it through. (Well, actually, pretty much all fighter pilots think that.) The friend I met during the training, Larry, got the same assignment, and we traveled together.

Homestead Air Force Base, Florida

https://en.wikipedia.org/wiki/Homestead_Air_Reserve_Base

January 1972

Water Survival Training

Before heading for an operational assignment after all this training, more training was needed. First, we had to go to Homestead AFB, FL, south of Miami, for water survival training. That was several days of academics plus pool training with the raft and other equipment.

The last part was at sea, well, Biscayne Bay, which is big enough that you are out of sight of the shore. We wore our flight suits, but they allowed us to wear tennis shoes instead of fight boots. It would ruin a pair of boots to wear them.

At sea, we were dangled behind an old flat-topped landing craft using parachute cords and a standard parachute harness. We were lowered into the water and dragged as if the chute stayed inflated after landing. We learned to solve this situation both face down and face up and finished by disconnecting the harness from the parachute cords, leaving us floating in our under-arm life preserver units (LPUs).

A speedboat then picked each of us up using the high-speed catch ring without slowing down. The ring is like a hula hoop. That's a bit exciting in itself! The speedboat delivered us back to the landing craft.

Then, we were each hooked to a parasail with a long rope. A speedboat towed us one at a time off the flat boat and a few hundred feet into the air. It was like launching from a mini aircraft carrier using a parasail.

31

We each had a one-man survival raft attached to our harness by a nylon rope and still wore the inflated LPU. The bag that holds the survival kit was also attached as if it had been deployed in an ejection, but it was empty. This was just like we would have after ejecting from an aircraft except without the main survival kit contents.

The fun started when I pushed the two levers that detached me from the tow rope. That put me in a parachute descent with the raft dangling below me. I landed in the water and climbed into the raft. That was easier than I expected, certainly due to the training in the pool. Here is a video of Water Survival Training. https://www.youtube.com/watch?v=OWt78Z5UdT8

Next, a UH-1 "Huey" helicopter was supposed to pick each of us up using the cable and winch. That's where things went seriously wrong.

Survival Training Got Real

The helicopter picked up a couple of guys, then the cable winch jammed. It had to fly to Homestead for repairs. Then, when it returned, the winch jammed again. This time, it also needed to refuel.

However, a large thunderstorm arrived at the base, and refueling was stopped due to lightning. During the storm, they determined that they couldn't fix the winch, so the boats would have to pick us up.

Of course, the storm was now over the bay. It was dark as night with torrential rain and high wind. That gave us six-foot waves for our four-foot rafts, and the rain was very cold. The three rescue boats couldn't see more than a few feet and had to stop moving for fear of running over someone.

Constant streaks of lightning while sitting in a one-man raft in the water is really intense! There were three consecutive severe thunder storms that took a total of two hours to pass over us.

We couldn't see each other or anything else, so we were now in a **REAL** survival situation. The high waves and wind blew us miles apart and well out of sight of shore. I didn't see the shore for so long that I thought I might have been blown out to sea!

We now had over 30 guys in one-man rafts freezing and scattered all over the large bay with the sun disappearing in the west. Most of the rafts capsized. Due to the waves, the guys couldn't get back in until the storms passed, but everyone was tied to their raft with the rope attached to their harness.

In the classroom, we had learned about a sea anchor. When the waves got high, I quickly used the rope to tie the raft bag into a scoop that could function as a sea anchor. I tied the other end of the rope to the front of the raft. That kept me facing with the waves, so I never capsized. I had a cold, violent, but upright ride for two hours. One or two other guys thought of the same thing.

When the storms passed, the boats started looking for us and picking guys up one by one. We had no signaling devices, so it was strictly a visual search. Unfortunately, the sun had set, so it was getting dark fast.

They found guys from a few hundred yards to over five miles off shore. I was one of those farthest from shore. They found me after full darkness using a searchlight. I was either the second or third from last one picked up.

When the boats got to the pier, they lined us up and counted to make sure we were all accounted for. When they were sure, they announced that, since we were all alive, we had passed water survival training!

Little did I know that this training would save my life within two years. I suppose this should count as Departure Crash #2.

Fairchild AFB, Washington

https://en.wikipedia.org/wiki/Fairchild_Air_Force_Base

March 1972

Basic Survival School

Next, Larry and I went to Basic Survival School at Fairchild AFB, WA. That was two weeks learning all the basic skills of survival, evasion, first aid, how to handle being a POW, how to use all the equipment, etc. It was April in Washington, so the woods were mostly still snow covered.

This was great training on how to use all the survival gear we had in the ejection seat kit. It also included instruction on how to live in desert, forest, or arctic conditions. Receiving over a foot of snow while sleeping in the tents we made of parachute sections added to the realism. I still remember how to prepare a rabbit for cooking.

During my career, I had to live at various times in tents in desert, swamp, tropical, and arctic conditions. Much of this training was useful even without it being in survival situations. Of course, simply living in a small tent in Alaska at minus 65F was tougher than survival training.

Bad trip to Korea

After surviving survival training, we headed to Travis AFB, CA, for our trip across the Pacific to Kunsan AB on a Boeing 720B, the long-range version of the 707. The flight stopped to refuel at Anchorage, Alaska, and was planned to refuel at Tokyo, Japan, before proceeding to Osan AB, at Seoul, South Korea.

Three-fourths of the way to Tokyo, Larry and I noticed that we rolled into 30 degrees of left bank and stayed that way for two minutes. All pilots would understand that to mean that we had just made a left 180-degree turn! It was *way* too late to turn back, so we started trying to figure out what was going on.

We quickly calculated that the time of flight would put us at our closest point to Russia. Oh, no! We must have accidentally flown into Russia and were trying to get out before getting intercepted!

In a few minutes, the pilot came on the PA and said: "Some of you might have noticed that we reversed course." Larry and I started emphatically nodding "yes". Then the pilot explained that we never got approval for the high altitude requested and found headwinds stronger than forecast; so, we didn't have enough fuel to reach Tokyo safely.

We turned back east for half an hour to land at Shemya AFB, Alaska, to refuel. We all had to get off the plane for refueling. Shemya is an interesting place. It's a flat, little island 200 miles from Russia, second from the end of the Aleutian Islands Chain. This was before the Cobra Dane early warning radar was built there.

All it had was a hangar for two RC-135 planes, a tower built for 150-mph wind (although they said they evacuate it a few times each year at 100 mph), and a few very low wooden buildings whose roofs extended all the way to the ground. A sign said the record high temperature was 52F and the record low was 20F. The wind was rarely below 30 knots. There were small sand drifts across the runway. Between the buildings were wooden walkways with handrails.

By the time we got to Tokyo, the crew didn't have enough crew rest to go further, so we had to spend the night there. We were all taken to the Hilton in downtown Tokyo in tiny buses that were designed to fit Japanese people. We folded ourselves into our seats and tried to see the sights as much as possible.

The next morning, we crammed into the tiny buses again, returned to the airport, and flew to Osan AB, Korea.

Osan Air Base, South Korea

https://en.wikipedia.org/wiki/Osan_Air_Base

April 1972

An F-4D that I flew

Surprise News at Osan

We had to spend a night at Osan AB before the next flight to Kunsan AB. While there, we ran into a guy who had been in our F-4 class. All our orders said was "8th Tactical Fighter Wing" (TFW) which had its headquarters at Kunsan AB. The wing had two squadrons at Kunsan AB on the middle west coast of South Korea and one squadron at Osan AB just south of Seoul.

He told us we were in the 35th Tactical Fighter Squadron (TFS). I asked, "Are they at Kunsan or Osan." He answered, "They're at Da Nang."

What?

While we were enroute on March 31, 1972, the North Vietnamese launched the "Easter Offensive" across the Demilitarized Zone (DMZ), turning Vietnam into a full-scale war with a front. The USAF deployed several fighter squadrons to fight it.

The 35th was the first to go, deploying on April 1, 1972. There is a whole other story about having a silent recall at 0500 on April Fool's Day, but I wasn't there to witness it.

So much for a safe assignment! This turned out to be the start of the heaviest air battles and bombing in the Vietnam War.

There was no Internet or e-mail in those days. It could take a week to schedule a $3 per minute long distance call to the USA. The squadron would be flying combat missions in Vietnam several days while their families still thought they were in Korea.

F-4D Training

Since the 8th TFW flew the F-4D, Larry and I were kept in Korea to learn the differences from the F-4C and get a combat type tactical check ride (Tac Check). We signed in at Kunsan, got barracks rooms, and spent one night there including unpacking our hold baggage boxes.

Then, we were sent to Osan AB, where we lived in the air defense alert facility for six weeks while flying the F-4D around Korea and honing our bombing and air-to-air combat skills.

I must admit, the fact that in just a few weeks you are certain to be flying combat into the best defended area since WWII makes you take training *very* seriously!

Arrival Crash #4

The day we were at Kunsan, an F-4D on a training flight at Osan had an engine fire. The procedure is to immediately shut down the engine with the illuminated fire light. The pilot did so. The fire light stayed on. Then, the other engine fire light came on. The pilot of the other F-4 in the flight confirmed heavy smoke from the bottom of the aircraft.

As flames began to envelope the entire aircraft, they ejected successfully over rice paddies about a mile short of the Osan runway.

The investigation could not determine the cause of the fire. However, they determined that, during maintenance several months earlier, the fire lights had been wired backward. That caused the pilot to shut down the good engine. We had to stand all F-4's at Osan down for a day while they were all inspected.

No Way Down?

The most serious emergency I had up to that point was during this training. One flight at Osan was a 4-ship, which, due to the weather, was planned as high-altitude air-to-air intercept practice. Clouds were solid from 300 feet to 35,000 feet, not unusual in Korea. We planned to take off with 20-second spacing and maintain 3-mile trail formation using radar while making a left turn to south and climbing.

Delaying your takeoff in an F-4 20 seconds behind the guy ahead ends up with 3 miles of spacing when you are up to the standard 300 knot join-up speed. I was number 2. After getting above the clouds, we planned to split into two 2-ship elements and run intercepts on each other under control of a Weapons Controller at a Ground Control Intercept (GCI) radar site.

Right after takeoff, my radar failed completely. Since we had already entered the clouds and I now had no way to maintain safe spacing, I delayed the turn a couple of miles to be sure to stay clear and kept climbing while my WSO worked the radar problem.

At the same time, I called Lead to tell him my problem. No answer. My radio was dead, too. Also, our TACAN navigation system was just spinning instead of pointing to Osan. I quickly saw that our air traffic control radar transponder was not operating, and our standby ten-channel radio wasn't working either. We had almost complete electrical failure.

Luckily, the cockpit intercom and the Inertial Navigation System (INS) seemed to work, but the F-4 INS is not very accurate. Its calculated location drifts a mile every 20 minutes. Basic heading and gyro instruments that operate off the INS still worked, so I could keep circling until getting above the clouds.

We finally got into clear blue sky above a 35,000' solid cloud deck, but were all alone with no usable navigation system, so we had no way to get back down.

Back then, the Instrument Flight Rules (IFR) Supplement book had a communication out procedure to signal radar controllers that you need assistance. You could fly triangles with two-minute legs. One direction meant just communication out, and the other direction meant communication and navigation equipment out. My WSO looked up the procedure in the book, and we used it. This procedure is no longer in the book, and I've never heard of anyone else using it.

I can't remember which way was which, but I started flying appropriate triangles (clockwise, I think) and moved a bit south to make sure we didn't fly into North Korea. We slowed to our best endurance speed to make our fuel last as long as possible.

We also discussed what to do when our fuel got low. We decided that we would go west long enough to be sure to be well off shore over the Yellow Sea. We could descend to a few hundred feet and carefully go lower using the radar altimeter. Oops. That wasn't working either.

That left us only the option to very carefully try to find the water visually. If we could fly west to go away from the coast and get low enough to see the water, then we could find Kunsan, since it's right at the shore.

Otherwise, we would climb back to 35,000' feet and continue triangles until we ran out of fuel. Then, we would use the INS to make sure the plane was headed out to sea, glide to a lower altitude, and eject. We didn't know that the clouds now went all the way down to 100 feet.

After half an hour of triangles, we saw a black F-4 smoke trail coming toward us from the south. A GCI controller had seen the skin paint of an unidentified aircraft doing triangles and connected it with the report of a missing plane from Osan. It was the GCI site that we were going to work with for our training.

Flight Lead sent 3 and 4 off to do their training and had the GCI vector him to intercept us, getting some of his planned training, too. He joined up on my left wing.

I gave him the standard signal for electrical failure, a clenched fist followed by two fingers. (HEFOE signal – 1 finger for Hydraulic, 2 for Electrical, 3 for Fuel, 4 for Oxygen, 5 for Engine.) Then, I signaled for him to take the lead.

With a huge feeling of relief, I tucked into close formation on Lead's right wing to go home. He patted his shoulder, the "follow me" signal.

I was expecting him to lead me through a weather penetration to Osan followed by a Ground Controlled Approach (GCA) where he would go around when the runway was in sight, and I would land first. With no radio, I had no way to know that the weather had deteriorated to 100-foot ceiling and one-fourth mile visibility with heavy rain in a thunderstorm.

As we stabilized onto final approach with gear and flaps down, I stacked level with Lead just as I trained during several previous

38

formation approaches. We were in heavy rain and, with no radar altimeter, I couldn't determine decision height (100 feet) perfectly but expected to see the runway much earlier than 100 feet.

Suddenly, I saw the runway and realized that we were about to touch down in a formation landing! Lead wanted to get both of us on the ground, because the weather might close the field at any time. I touched down exactly with Lead in perfect position, popped my drag chute, and touched the brakes to drop behind Lead. It was a perfect formation landing. While rolling down the runway, I told my WSO that this was my first formation landing. He yelled, "Why didn't you tell me?" I replied, "It would have just made you nervous."

At this point, I might mention that all my previous practice formation approaches were actually low approaches without landing. Tactical Air Command (TAC) had suspended student formation landings while I was in training while they investigated an incident where a student dinged wingtips with his leader. Back in UPT, students never did formation landings. We did ride through one with the IP flying to familiarize us with what it looks like.

After getting back to the squadron, I told Lead that was my first formation landing. He nearly fainted. Then, he said, "Great job." and signed off formation landing on my training record.

Later, at Korat, we did formation landings routinely to get large numbers of planes on the ground in minimum time.

Almost Departure Crash #3

After six weeks of flying every day, my final training flight was a Tac Check. I was #2 in a 2-ship with an IP Check Pilot leading. We went to the Koon Ni bombing range south of Osan. We did standard 10, 30, and 45 degree bombing, 30 degree rockets, and 10-degree strafing. I qualified in all events.

Then we flew an intercept on another pair of F-4s and engaged them in some air combat maneuvering. That ended in a draw as both of us displayed better defense than offense. Since the opposing pilot was experienced, a draw was good.

Finally, we did some unscripted road reconnaissance with Lead picking out targets and me setting up to attack them. After doing that for a few minutes, I was at Bingo fuel and called "Two is Bingo" on the radio. (That's the planned amount for heading home.). Lead said, "Roger" and kept picking targets. When I was 300 pounds below

Bingo, I called "Bingo minus 3." About five minutes later, my next call was, "Two is Bingo minus 8, and I need to head for base."

The Check Pilot leading finally turned toward Osan. The rules were to arrive over the field with 1,500 pounds or call "min fuel." Tower would then give you priority, but it looks bad that you got so low. At 1,200 pounds, a required "emergency fuel" call must be made. An F-4D uses about 100 pounds per minute in cruise and 400 in afterburner. By this time, I was down to 1,300 pounds.

Lead landed first with me on final approach a few seconds behind. However, as I was on short final, a Korean C-46 pulled onto the runway to takeoff right behind Lead without being cleared. Suddenly, instead of my landing spot, all I could see was this huge, twin engine cargo plane filling my windscreen! (Just like the dust devil in UPT)

I slammed the throttles to full afterburner and pulled up, barely missing the huge vertical tail. I can't imagine what the Korean pilots thought when my pair of F-4 afterburners passed a few feet over their heads with the burner flame pointed right at their windscreen, or what the tower controller said to them later. Amazingly, that dust devil at Laredo had trained me for just this situation!

As soon as I got a good climb started, I pulled it out of afterburner and looked at my fuel. It said 800 pounds. I called tower, declared emergency fuel, and said I was leaving my landing gear down and doing a left 360 degree turn to land.

It was non-standard, but tower cleared me immediately. I landed, immediately shut down the left engine, and taxied to my parking shelter. I shut down with 300 pounds.

I wasn't at all happy at the debrief, but I shut up since I just wanted to get the Tac Check signed off and be done with it. The IP finally apologized for running me so low on fuel that there was no margin for problems.

Finally, Larry and I completed our TAC checks and were ready to head for Vietnam. As final preparation for the war, we were sent to the Philippines for jungle survival training on the way.

Clark Air Base, Philippines

https://en.wikipedia.org/wiki/History_of_Clark_Air_Base

May 1972

Jungle Survival Training

L   arry and I were given orders to proceed to Clark AB, Philippines, and get into the next Jungle Survival School class, then join our squadron at Da Nang AB, Vietnam. We got seats on what everyone called the "3-holer." That was a contract Boeing 727 (3 engines) that flew to all the main bases from northern Japan to the Philippines every other day. It would go north one day and south the next day.

We got to Clark two hours after a four-day class started, so they made us wait four days to get into the next class. What a hardship! We had to kill our first four days ever in the Philippines doing whatever we wanted. That meant sightseeing from busses and trying out the illegal casino owned by the Deputy Mayor. I actually won a few bucks.

Then, it was off to the camp at the base of Mount Pinatubo. The jungle is a totally different world. No plants, insects, or animals were familiar, and many can kill you. I was amazed to learn that the ear splitting screech that you hear all night long is made by a one-inch frog!

Hiding from Negritos

I took Jungle Survival very seriously to learn all I could. I was one of the very few who managed to hide so well that the Negritos didn't find me. Negritos are pygmy tribesmen who live in remote areas of the Philippines. They are about 4 feet tall, medium dark skinned, wear only loincloths, and carry a spear. At least this described them in 1972.

They carried a card with drawings of an eye, ear, and nose to point to the way they found us. We each had a red dog tag that we had to give to them when we were found. They got paid with a bag of rice for each tag they turned in. They had so much fun tracking us down that they hated to see the class end. Or maybe that was because of the rice.

We had to hide twice, once in the morning and once in the afternoon. The Negritos had two hours to find us each time. The first time, I was found shortly before time expired.

The second time, I found an area where bamboo stalks were all laying almost horizontal. I laid on my back and slid under them. They were so thick, I couldn't see out. I laid there the whole time wondering what other creatures might be under there with me. I listened intently so that I could hear anything coming and get out. I drank some water

41

and ate an energy bar while there. This time, the Negritos couldn't find me. Luckily, no critter wanted to share my energy bar.

The Bat Cave

On our first day in the jungle, we were in a large ravine at the base of Mount Pinatubo. This active volcano had earthquakes quite often, and the result is large cracks in the Earth. We came across an area of large slabs of rock that were leaning on each other at various angles. One place made a triangular opening that stood about five feet high by five feet across at the bottom. Shining flashlights in there did not show a bottom.

One guy threw a baseball sized rock in. We never heard it hit bottom. He tried a softball sized one with the same result. Then, our instructor threw a football sized rock in. We still did not hear it hit anything. Then we started hearing a "whoosh, whoosh" sound and the instructor yelled, "Get back!" Seconds later, a vampire bat with about a two-foot wingspan came flying out right over our heads.

Giant Rats

We were warned about rats the size of cats that could get into our gear and food if not put out of their reach. For sleeping, we made hammocks out of parachute sections and strung them between small trees. There was a three-foot high tree stump just within arm reach of my hammock. I decided to take my boots off and sit them there after laying down.

In the total darkness of the jungle, I had to reach out and sit them on the stump by feel. Seconds after I put them there, one fell off. I didn't have the nerve to put my feet down in the dark to get it, so I went to sleep, wondering when the bat would return to the bat cave.

I woke up to a gnawing sound. I clapped my hands, and heard a rat scampering away. This went on several times. I was sure that my boot would be in shreds by morning.

When morning came, I found out that the rat had been gnawing on a root at the foot of the tree where the head of my hammock was tied. What a relief! Also, we didn't see the bat again.

Changed Destination Again

We had reservations on a C-141 to go to Da Nang the day we came in from the camp, but a sign taped on our room door said we were cancelled. We called the Command Post and were told our squadron had left Da Nang and was now split between Ubon AB, and Korat AB, both in Thailand, and they had to decide where we should go.

The next day, they said the entire squadron was going to assemble at Korat, so we got a hop on a C-141 to Korat. It was carrying the two of us plus several pallets of "Stars and Stripes" newspapers that we dropped off (by landing) at various bases along the way.

Clark AB 19 years later with Pinatubo erupting

Fate of Clark AB

About 19 years after I left, Mount Pinatubo blew up, destroying the survival school and most of the main base with falling ash. The volcano gave several days of warning activity before erupting, so the base was evacuated.

The photo is Pinatubo exploding the other side of Clark AB and a farmer working his field in the foreground. Well, there wasn't a crash after I left, but the whole base was destroyed! The survival school jungle area was buried. A runway and a few buildings have now been restored and the base is a civilian air field.

Map of Southeast Asia

North Vietnam Route Packs

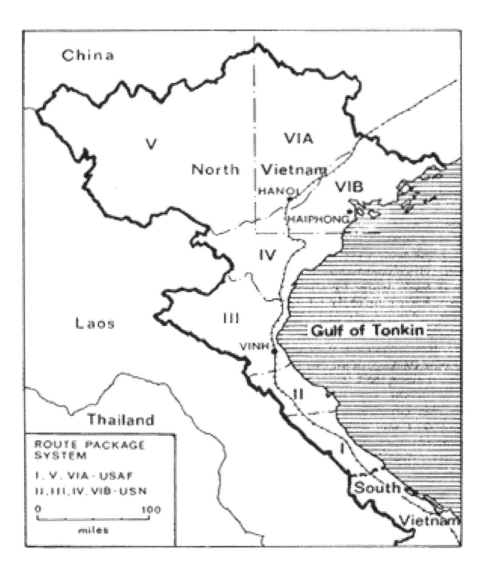

Korat Royal Thai Air Base, Thailand

https://en.wikipedia.org/wiki/Korat_Royal_Thai_Air_Force_Base

May 1972

F-4E

Enemy In a Boot

When the first 35th Tactical Fighter Squadron guys arrived at Korat, they were billeted in empty bunks with units scattered all over Korat. Right after I arrived, they decided to move the 35th TFS members all together.

There was an army camp attached to Korat called Camp Friendship. It had been abandoned for a few years. They gave us a 2-story barracks for our enlisted men and put the officers into what had been the colonel's quarters for the Army.

They put three of our officers into each room by adding two beds. The nice thing was that each room had its own bathroom. The permanent AF aircrews lived in flimsy shacks with 4-man rooms and a common bathroom in a separate shack. Our maintenance personnel were put into an old 2-story barracks across the street.

While abandoned, the Camp Friendship officer's area had become overrun with cobras. For us to move in, they hired several Thai men and paid them five Baht for each one they caught. That's about a dollar. Each one of them caught several dozen snakes.

A couple of days later, a guy in the room next to me went to get out of bed in the morning and found a baby Cobra in one of his boots! He beat it to death with his other boot. Our first enemy kill.

Then, we learned nature's food chain there. It seems that the Cobras eat baby frogs. With no Cobras, we had a plague of millions of baby frogs. They covered the ground. Every step squashed a few. To go into our rooms, we had to sweep them away from the door with our foot and hurry inside. Then, we had to catch the five to ten that got in and throw them out the window.

Thousands would gather in a concrete culvert under the road outside our windows and croak in unison. Imagine thousands of frogs making high pitched screeches through a powerful amplifier.

Of course, that would be while we were trying to sleep.

There were so many frogs that nearly all died within a few days. What a stench!

Frogs eat mosquitoes. Now, the frogs were gone. Amazingly, none of us got malaria from the clouds of mosquitoes.

Arrival Crash #5

Larry and I arrived at Korat just in time for two celebrations. One was for the arrival of one of our squadron crews who had been shot down just off the North Vietnamese coast two days previously and picked up by the Navy.

The other was for our squadron commander shooting down a MiG-21 that day. The squadron shot down a total of 1 MiG-17 and 15 MiG-21's during the 7-month deployment.

While not actually crashing, my new flight commander, Charlie, had his two racks of six MK-82's (500-pound bombs) drop off his F-4 just after takeoff. They tumbled a few times, then three bombs detonated, It put holes in a couple of parked F-105's and wounded a crew chief. Welcome to the combat zone!!! Will this kind of thing happen everywhere I go?

SA-7 Downs an F-4

Several days earlier, Denny, my roommate at Korat, had the honor of being the WSO in the first jet shot down by an SA-7 missile in combat.

They were number 2 in a 2-ship working a Close Air Support (CAS) target east of Quang Tri. They had some of the last CBU-14s in the inventory. It dumps little bomblets out the back of six tubes. It's really made for a slower plane like the A-1. The bomblets are incendiary.

They hit NVN troops with the bomblets in a low pass at the maximum delivery speed for this munition of 450 knots. Often, a bomblet sticks in a tube, so you jettison the tubes before landing. The jettison is to be done below 400 knots so that it doesn't hit the wing. The pilot decided to jettison over the target since they didn't know where friendlies might be.

The SA-7 Strella was the first hand-held heat-seeker anti-aircraft missile. The Russians had just deployed it and provided some to NVN. We knew that a jet moving faster than 450 knots can't be caught by an SA-7 due to its very short range, but no one knew there might be an SA-7 in the area. None had been seen, yet.

On their jettison pass, an SA-7 was fired from their 5 o'clock position. It hit between the tailpipes, blowing the tail section off the F-4D. The plane went into a flat spin, and they had to eject without being sure they were away from the NVN forces. Both got out uninjured.

The pilot landed in an open area where several soldiers formed a circle while he landed in the center of the circle. Of course, there were no Americans on the ground there, so all he heard was the soldiers yelling excitedly in Vietnamese. Since they had just hit the target troops with incendiaries, he thought he would be shot on sight at best.

To his surprise, they ran to him, helped him to his feet and said, "Friend. Friend." Their F-4 had just missed crashing into the friendlies.

Meanwhile, Denny landed in a stand of elephant grass in a slight ravine. He tucked under it and hid as best he could. He heard Vietnamese troops approaching, searching in the elephant grass. All he could think of was the training video from survival school of enemy troops jabbing their bayonets into high grass and bushes while searching for a downed pilot.

Suddenly, a pair of hands parted the grass in front of him and a face smiled and said, "Friend." The SVN soldiers who found them walked them about five miles to an M113 Armored Personnel Carrier. Then, they got a ride to a spot where a SVN Huey picked them up and took them to Da Nang. They were back at Korat the next day.

Ready for Combat

Here I am ready for a LINEBACKER mission into North Vietnam in 1972. The above photo is an F-4E dropping Mk-82 (500 lb.) bombs (usually 12) in a 45-degree dive over North Vietnam.

Chuck, June 1972

As an FNG (F...ing New Guy), I first flew a few close air support (CAS) missions into South Vietnam. Those went well. My dive bombing accuracy was often complemented by the Forward Air Controller (FAC). I saw a little anti-aircraft artillery (AAA or "Triple A") fire, 23mm, 37mm, 57mm. You can't see the small arms and most machine gun fire, since they usually don't use tracer ammo and the rounds don't explode in the air.

My squadron had the F-4D. We flew those on bombing missions. The rest of Korat had E models. Those were used for all the air-to-air missions because they had more thrust, turned better, and had a built-in 20mm gun that fired 100 rounds per second.

It was decided that we could fly the E because it was easier to fly than a D but used different techniques. The Korat guys were not allowed to fly our Ds. The D had tricky takeoff procedures and you couldn't use aileron to roll when pulling G's due to adverse yaw. All high-G turning required using only rudder. E pilots would probably spin it during a SAM break or air-to-air combat! As a result, my squadron flew far more bombing missions than air-to-air.

Something like 60 F-4C & Ds were lost in spins over the years the Air Force had them.

First Mission North

My sixth mission was my first into North Vietnam (NVN). The target was three fuel storage tanks near Dong Hoi in the southern part of NVN (Route Pack 1). I was number 2 in a 4-ship, each carrying 12 MK-82s (500-pound bombs). It was to be a 45-degree dive bomb attack releasing at 12,000 feet with each of us aiming at specific tanks.

Approaching the target, we didn't see any AAA. There were the white fuel tanks and clear sky. We rolled in from 18,000'. I lined up my bomb sight just short of the tanks so the target would be centered when I reached 12,000'. A couple of seconds before the release point, my target disappeared behind a solid cloud of small, puffy, black clouds.

AAA!!! The gunners were filling my flight path with AAA fire! I rolled hard right, turned with 5 Gs, jerked the stick back left, pulled it to go around the cloud, and ended up dropping the bombs maybe a quarter of a mile past the target. That was my first experience with heavy defensive fire. In later missions, I got the hang of dodging the AAA and still hitting the target.

An Loc Tank Kill

https://www.reddit.com/r/DestroyedTanks/comments/4c5eb2/north _vietnamese_t54_caught_in_a_b52_raid/

The NVN army laid siege to the town of An Loc for 2 months and attacked over and over. There were about 30 American Army and Marine advisors trapped there with the SVN forces surrounded by NVN forces.

CAS is all that kept the base from being overrun. Ammo and food were also dropped by air. A C-130 even dropped a 30,000 pound bomb to collapse the NVN tunnels and to blow away their tree cover. The

NVN Army led the attacks with Russian made T-54 tanks, the biggest use of tanks in the war.

On May 12, 1972, I was in a 2-ship flight tasked for CAS there. We contacted a Covey FAC who was over the area in an O-2 controlling numerous fighters. When our turn came, he pointed out a tank that was firing into the friendly positions.

We each had 12 Mk-82's. It pretty much takes a direct hit to take out a tank, so he suggested that we drop them in "trips" (3 at a time).

We started making passes. Lead strung his first 3 across the tank landing one on each side. The tank disappeared into the black smoke from the bomb explosions. Within a few seconds, we saw the tank drive out of the smoke, swing its turret back towards the friendlies, and fire its main gun.

I did the same with my pass with the same results. We both made a second pass with the same results again. The three guys in that tank must have been deaf by now but seemed determined to keep shooting.

Lead dropped his third trip and missed. I rolled in for the third time. This time, one of my bombs scored a direct hit into the right side of the tank! When the black smoke from the bomb cleared, the tank was leaning with its left side in a crater and the rear was on fire. The FAC said the guys in the command bunker were yelling and cheering! They told him that tank had been shooting at the door of the command bunker. We saved them all.

Several years later, I met two of the US Army officers who were in that bunker. One was at Fort Hood, and one was while working for CACI after I retired from the AF. I'll cover Fort Hood later.

They told me that killing that tank really turned the battle. The NVN were closing in from all sides and the friendly officers were forced to retreat into one of the few remaining bunkers. All 17 of the surviving Americans and all the SVN Army leadership for that area were in the bunker.

The troops outside were hunkered down but couldn't fight back effectively. That tank could have killed them all. This was the only time I attacked a tank. I don't know for sure, but a photo of a destroyed T-54 at An Loc looks exactly like I remember the tank I hit the last time I saw it. It was leaning into the crater in exactly this manner, but I don't have permission to include it.

https://www.reddit.com/r/DestroyedTanks/comments/4c5eb2/north _vietnamese_t54_caught_in_a_b52_raid/

In 1998, six years after retiring from the Air Force, I was working for CACI on a war simulation computer program in Rosslyn, VA. A retired Army colonel who I worked with was talking to me one day, and we realized that we had been in Vietnam at the same time.

He mentioned that he had been at An Loc, so I said that I had supported that battle a couple of times and killed a tank there. We both went over the events and realized that he was one of the Americans in that bunker.

He told me that he had destroyed two tanks at An Loc with Light Antitank Weapon (LAW) missiles. He also mentioned that they wondered why the crews never got out of a burning tank. After the battle, they looked into the tanks and found that the 3-man crews were all chained to their seats. That's why they were so persistent even when many were being destroyed.

He said there was a reunion coming up for An Loc survivors, and it was being held in Rosslyn, VA, so he asked me to attend. Barbara and I went and met eight survivors and their wives. The other nine had either died or were unable to travel. There were lots of war stories. They had enlarged photos of previous reunions posted around the room. We had a great time.

The next day, we held a ceremony at the Vietnam War Memorial in DC. We all wore hats that said "An Loc Warrior." We formed up at attention while the senior officer read the list of names of those who were killed and those who had died since. The amazing part of this was the crowd reaction.

There are always quite a few people in that area. Some of them stopped near us. Most came to attention. More and more kept joining. When the list was finished, there were about 50 people there. They all applauded, and most shook our hands and thanked us for our service.

The reunions were every two years. The next one was in New Orleans, but I didn't travel to it. After that, there were only two survivors still in good enough physical condition to travel, so they stopped the reunions. I still have my hat.

Night Combat

Nearly half of my missions were night. I was quite happy flying at night, mainly because the AAA guns mostly used tracers. 85mm and 100mm guns did not use tracers, but they were radar guided. We had radar warning devices, so we knew if they were tracking us. Also, it takes 5 to 10 seconds for the round to get from the gun to the aircraft, so if you just jink (quickly change direction a small amount) every 5 seconds, the radar can't predict where to shoot.

14.7mm machine guns had green tracers. Twin 23mm guns used red tracers every fifth round with a high rate of fire. It looked like two parallel fire hoses spraying red water. 37 and 57mm guns had an orange tracer on every round and fired clips of four to seven rounds. We would see strings of orange balls each time they fired, and reloading took up to 10 seconds. Tracers made it possible to simply dodge the fire.

CAS at night presented another problem. We liked to leave our lights off when low over the enemy at night for obvious reasons. Passing low directly over the target and pulling up into a climb is the time you are most vulnerable to ground fire of all types. However, the FAC is required to see that the fighter is aimed at the correct target before clearing it to drop. FACs insisted that we keep some light on, usually the red rotating beacon on top, until they called "Cleared hot."

That meant setting up for the attack and rolling in on the target with the light still on. The F-4 exterior light switches are halfway up the right side of the front cockpit slightly behind the pilot's right elbow where it's impossible to reach with your left hand due to being strapped into the ejection seat.

You fly with your right hand on the stick between your legs and left hand on the throttles. A bomb run requires constant adjustment of both.

At the "cleared hot" call, we had to let go of the throttles, continue lining up on the target using the left hand on the stick, twist the right arm to where we could reach and feel the switch, turn it off, switch hands back, and press the button to drop the bombs, all while attaining the correct airspeed, altitude, and dive angle to hit the target.

Due to the close proximity of friendlies in a CAS situation, if you were too slow getting lined up, you had to go through dry and make another pass. A wasted pass can get the ground troops in trouble due to lack of support and puts the fighter at risk for the additional pass.

Looking Down the Barrel

One night, we were working with a FAC trying to hit NVN troops along a river east of Quang Tri. We were being harassed by sporadic AAA from 37mm and twin 23mm guns scattered around the area.

We had all external lights off, so they were shooting at sound or just guessing. The 37mm tracers don't ignite until 2,000 feet after they leave the barrel, and the barrels have very good flash suppressors, so it's hard to pinpoint the gun position.

Suddenly, one of the 37's fired with the gun aimed directly at me. Of course, the rounds went well behind me, but I saw the muzzle flash. It was in the center of a small horseshoe the river made.

I told the FAC "Two has one of the 37's spotted." He immediately said, "Hit it with the rest of your bombs!" I still had 6 Mk-82's with daisy cutters (18-inch fuse extenders). I put them directly on the gun position. The daisy cutters cause the shrapnel to spread out flat across the ground instead of up out of a crater, covering a larger area.

There were some secondary explosions and a pretty good sustained fire. No more AAA came from that position, and the other guns fired less. A FAC in the area the next day reported the 37mm gun laying on its side with the barrel bent.

OV-10 FAC Down

On another night mission, we were supposed to work with a Nail FAC. Nails flew OV-10 aircraft. We arrived in the area east of Quang Tri near the coast carrying 12 Mk-82's each. Lead called the FAC and reported on station. There was a flight of F-4's already there.

The Lead of that flight answered with "FAC's taken a hit. He's on fire. He's trying to get feet wet." He was trying to get offshore before ejecting. Just as we arrived, we saw a flash about 5 miles offshore and a large explosion several seconds later. Those were his ejection seat and then the OV-10 crashing into the water. He didn't have anyone in the back seat. We found out later that he had been hit in a tailpipe by an SA-7 missile.

We couldn't see him in his raft in the dark, but enemy arty started firing into his area. The arty guns made a smoke cloud each time they fired. We used our bombs on the arty positions and shut them down.

An SVN Army Huey flew out and picked up the FAC. It took him to Da Nang, and we headed back to Korat.

First Confirmed KBA

I was #2 in a 2-ship daytime flight sent to a southern area of SVN to work with a FAC in an O-2. It was in an open area of rice paddies with a canal through the middle. The FAC pointed out a grass hooch along the canal with a tree on each side of it. Sitting in the canal next to the hooch was a sampan. The FAC said that men were offloading ammunition boxes from the sampan and putting them into the hooch. We could see a man standing in each end of the sampan.

Lead told me to go first, so I set up to attack with three Snakeyes (MK-82 bombs with high-drag fins that open up to slow it down fast). Since the bombs drop back quickly, they don't explode right under you, so you can use a 10 degree dive and 1,000 foot bomb release to be very accurate. I lined up to go straight over the sampan toward the hooch. I centered the sight just short of the hooch and pickled. I pulled out of the shallow dive with 5 Gs and rolled left for a sharp turn to avoid possible small arms fire.

Looking over my left shoulder, I saw the bombs impact. The first one hit the center of the sampan between the two standing guys. The second one hit the shore between the sampan and the hooch. The third went right into the hooch. That resulted in an impressive explosion that dwarfed the blast from the 500 pound Snakeyes. Apparently, there was quite a lot of explosives already in the hooch. As the smoke cleared, there was no sign of anything but craters.

The FAC was ecstatic and called the ground commander for another target for Lead to hit. He passed a Bomb Damage Assessment (BDA) reporting a destroyed sampan, a destroyed ammunition storage hooch, large secondary explosions, a sustained fire, and two confirmed Killed By Air (KBA). I'm sure that there were many more unconfirmed over seven months of hitting targets.

Battle of Kampong Trabaek

My most unusual CAS mission was in the town of Kampong Trabaek, near Cambodia east of the Mekong River right on the Kampong Trabaek river in South Vietnam.

I was #2 in a 2-ship of F-4D's sent to work with a Covey FAC. We were each carrying three 750-pound napalm cans on the centerline and 6 Snakeyes under our wings.

He was flying an O-2 and working a very complex target alone. When we arrived, the FAC put us into the top of the stack of fighters he was working. He assigned everyone to hold over a certain point within sight of the target area spaced 500 feet apart by altitude. When we arrived, there were at least eight 2-ship flights of F-4, A-4, A-7, A-37, A-1, and F-5 aircraft from the Air Force, Navy, Marines, and Vietnamese Air Force.

The FAC would have the bottom flight hit a target while the others descended 500 feet to the next lower orbit. It was extremely useful that all aircraft in the stack could hear the briefings and see a few other attacks before it was their turn.

At that time, the town was 90% east of the river with a bridge connecting to the west part. North Vietnamese troops had attacked from the east and taken the entire east part of the town. The fight had lasted a few days, and all civilians had fled.

The fight now was for the NVN forces to get across the bridge. SVN troops were trapped on the west side of a low stone wall about 200 meters west of the bridge. The NVN troops were continuously firing across the river at the friendlies.

Lead told me go to first. The FAC directed me to a 2-story building between the river and the road that parallels the river near the bridge. The roof was red tile with the crest parallel to the river. The crest was filled with NVN troops laying down and firing across the river over the peak of the roof. Several more were firing across the river out of the second-floor windows. Others were running in and out of the doors. They seemed to think they were safe there.

The FAC said, "Use your nape. Come in from the north endwise to the building."

I got a good look at the building and called the FAC, asking, "Is that a steeple on the building?"

The FAC said, "Yeah. It was a Catholic Church. Now, it's a Fortified Fighting Position and all civilians are gone."

That made it a legitimate target. I rolled in using a 10-degree dive and 1,000' release to get good accuracy. The first nape can hit the end of the first floor right into the door. The second one went into the end of the second floor. The third one hit the peak of the roof, covering the whole roof.

The FAC yelled, "Great hit, Two!" Then he said, "Lead, your target is the Buddhist Pagoda across the street. Do the same thing."

After similar results, the FAC said, "See that square park full of trees two blocks from the church?" We both saw it. The FAC said, "Soldiers have been running from your previous target area into that park. Use your Snakeyes and make an "X" from corner to corner in that square." We did exactly that. No one ran out of the park.

A couple of years later, I was an O-2 FAC and fully understood the incredible job that Covey did controlling that battle.

Took a Hit

On a mission into far south SVN, we worked a small infantry fight. There were no more than about 15 SVN soldiers shooting back and forth across a canal with Viet Cong fighters. We each had 6 Snakeyes and three 750-pound napalm canisters. Both are normally delivered from 1,000 feet in a 10-degree dive. We got good hits on the bad guys, and the SVN troops finished them off.

Lead and I checked each other over as usual, and all looked okay. After I parked and shut down back on the ramp at Korat, the crew chief, doing a quick post-flight of my plane, called me to the left side.

He showed me that one of the bomb racks under my left wing had been split in half by probably a 51-caliber machine gun bullet. Both halves were still there, but crooked. It must have happened after I released the Snakeye that had been on that station.

Otherwise, it would have hit the bomb and likely would have deflected into the bottom of the wing into a fuel tank. The result of that could have been different. This was the only hit I took while flying in Vietnam.

Enemy in the Cockpit

The heat and humidity at Korat in the summer was tough to handle. It was 95°F and 95% humidity most days. By the time we completed preflighting the aircraft and weapons, we would already be soaked when we climbed into the cockpit. On one large mission, we had route and target changes after engine start. We had to coordinate and rebrief the mission on the radio. That meant wearing the oxygen mask, since the microphone was in it. The mask fairly quickly filled with sweat.

We finally taxied out to the runway. On large missions, we would line up for takeoff four abreast with two or three 4-ship flights in trail. I was number 2 in the lead flight, so I was in the front row second from the left. We would start rolling one at a time with 12 seconds spacing. After stopping in takeoff position, I pulled one side of my mask off and poured the sweat out of it. As I went to put it back on, I saw movement in the mask. I held it up so I could see better and there was a big spider crawling around. It was brown and looked like what we called a Daddy Longlegs back in the States. I quickly shook it out onto the floor and stomped on it. I was able to get the mask back on and my hands on the controls just before Lead started rolling.

I wondered for a moment how I would explain the mess to the crew chief when I got back. Then, I started wondering how it would have gone if it had crawled onto my mouth during takeoff roll. I'm not sure how I would have handled that.

Then, I had to explain to my WSO what all the commotion was in the front cockpit. I thought he was going to hurt himself laughing. I decided that, on all future flights, I would blow air through the hose on the mask test machine a lot longer than I had before.

Destroyed SA-2 Site in Transit

I was in a 2-ship carrying 12 MK-82s each on a mission into RP 2 to work with a Wolf FAC. Lead was my new flight commander, Chuck. The FAC was circling over an old French rubber plantation. The plantation buildings were in the center of a rectangle of rubber trees about a mile east to west and a quarter of a mile north to south.

The FAC had been told that, due to very muddy conditions, an entire SA-2 SAM site had to stop moving the previous night and hid under the rubber trees. That's a great hiding place due to the huge leaves blocking the view of the ground from the air. There were vehicle tracks in the mud in various places around the plantation.

The FAC told us that he suspected that the SAM vehicles were parked east of the buildings in the trees. He had us drop three bombs at a time making north to south runs. After we used half our bombs, we still didn't see anything and didn't see any results from the bombs.

The FAC then said to put the next pass right in the east end of the trees. We were circling counter clockwise and I followed Lead around to the northeast to set up for the 30-degree dive pass we were using.

To my surprise, as we approached the east end of the trees, he didn't roll in. He kept going west and rolled in on the WEST end of the trees. I stayed high and didn't roll in.

A bigger surprise was the huge secondary explosions that Lead's bombs caused. The FAC started yelling, "I don't know what you saw, but you found it! Put the rest of your bombs in that area."

I still had six bombs, and Lead had three, so we kept hitting around the initial explosions. We got numerous explosions and fires as vehicles and missiles blew up. At one point, we saw a missile that looked like its engine was firing spinning around in circles, smashing other vehicles and missiles.

The FAC thanked us for the good work and gave us credit for destroying an entire SAM site. We never told him that Lead had misunderstood which end of the trees to hit. Blind luck.

Double and Triple Turn Missions

We flew some missions that were multiple flights. One was where we would launch from Korat with Snake and nape and fly a CAS mission in SVN, then land at Bien Hoa AB (12 miles NE of Saigon). We would refuel and rearm there and get a new mission. It would usually be another CAS. After that mission, we would return to Korat. I remember a large sign that was on the wall behind the duty desk in our Bien Hoa operations center. It was white with large red letters.

The other type would be an interdiction mission into RP 1 or 2

> **ROCKET ATTACK WARNING**
> **A LOUD EXPLOSION**
> **FOLLOWED BY A STEADY SIREN**

working with a Fast FAC. On these, we would land at Da Nang for fuel and weapons. Then, we would fly a very short mission with a Fast FAC in the same area. This could take as little as 20 minutes. That left time for another turn at Da Nang for another target before returning to Korat. I didn't fly any of those, but I did do double turns.

Rocket Attack at Da Nang

The second half of a double turn, we were taking off from Da Nang at night. We were taxiing south on the main taxiway half way to the end of the runway when we saw 5 sparkling streaks which were clearly rocket exhaust from 122mm rockets. They went from the ridgeline straight in front of us about 5 kilometers away straight up.

Except they weren't actually going straight up. It just looked like that, because they were angling straight toward us. We did all we could do – stop and run the seat full down to duck. All of them landed short of the perimeter fence, so we quickly taxied the rest of the way and took off.

Rocket Attacks at Bien Hoa

The Air Force always requires an F-4 pilot to be in the mobile control tower at any base where F-4's regularly operate. That is primarily for assistance when there are aircraft problems.

Bien Hoa did not have any F-4 pilots, so we took turns one week at a time. We would put some spare underwear, some socks, and a spare flight suit in a helmet bag and carry it in the cockpit on one of the Bien Hoa turn missions. Then we would swap with the guy who had been there for his week. There was one room in the one-story Marine officers barracks that was ours to use. One week in late summer, it was my turn.

Since it was hot with no air conditioning, most of us slept wearing little or nothing. I was sleeping soundly on my fifth night there. At 5AM, I woke to a series of 5 explosions. They usually launched 122mm rockets in volleys of 5. Another 5 followed in a few seconds.

There was a sod bunker just outside the barracks entrance, so I grabbed an armored vest and marine helmet and ran into the bunker. Rockets kept coming in volley after volley. Then, I heard outgoing artillery fire and small arms fire from the SVN Army and US Marines reacting.

Some of the rocket hits were quite close and shook dust loose from the ceiling. Of course, it was dark, and I hadn't paid much attention to the construction of the bunker during daylight. I also noticed that I was the only one in the bunker. I looked around and found that the bunker was made of cut sod stacked up for the sides and the roof was sod laid on old, bending boards. I realized that a nearby hit could collapse the whole thing on me.

I waited for the next short lull in incoming rounds and ran back to my room. The outer wall of the room was a two-foot tall concrete wall with wood above that, so I laid down under my bed against the concrete wall. The rockets kept coming for an hour with only 2 or 3 minute lulls at times.

When the attack ended, about 25 people had been wounded and one Marine was killed. He was walking between buildings collecting the money from the Orphan Fund boxes that were scattered around the base. One of the first rockets hit right next to him, so he never had a chance to take cover.

Most of those wounded were standing inside the air terminal building in the pay line to pick up their monthly pay. One of them had the motor half of a rocket stuck in his back. Amazingly, he survived. Another had the entire corner of the building collapse on top of him, but he was under his steel bed frame and was unhurt.

About 100 feet straight out the window from my room was a building that the Marines were using to maintain their 20mm guns. Some 20mm ammunition was in there.

The building took three hits and burned. 20mm rounds kept cooking off for a couple of hours. Firefighters arrived with a truck, but couldn't approach the building until the fire subsided.

One rocket just nicked the roof of the building next to me, causing it to hit the ground flat. That made it spray the shrapnel horizontal in addition to up.

After daylight, I went out and looked around. Shrapnel from the rocket that hit flat had hit the wall of my room. There were two nasty sharp pieces of shrapnel stuck in the wood between the concrete and the window. One is 2 inches long and the other is about ¾ inch. I managed to pry them out and have carried them in my work briefcase ever since for luck. Here is the large piece. You can see the diamond shaped scoring that makes it shatter into thousands of deadly pieces.

Another rocket hit the area behind the Base Exchange where all the cardboard cases of beer were stored and set it on fire. The fire caused cans of beer to keep exploding for a couple of hours. That *really* made the Marines mad!

A row of rocket craters in the blacktop aircraft parking ramp was right in front of a row of steel revetments where most of the aircraft fuel trucks were parked. All of the trucks had the front end torn up with radiators full of holes, front tires flat, and windshields blown out. None had the fuel tank punctured and none caught fire. If their aim had been 50 feet farther, there would have been an inferno.

During the attack, the Vietnamese tried to launch an AC-119 gunship, but while it was taxiing, a rocket landed under the wing and blew several feet of the wingtip off.

I found out later that the defense of the base had been turned over to the SVN Army the day before the attack. Previously, the US Marines had attack helicopters airborne all night watching the areas from which rockets could be launched and Marine ground patrols were ready to respond. The SVN Army did not have any patrols outside the perimeter at all.

While I was in the Snack Bar eating breakfast, there were several large explosions that caused a scramble for everyone to get under the tables. It was the Marines putting in an air strike just off the end of the runway where the rocket launchers were.

Several weeks later, Bien Hoa was hit by a rocket attack that hit the area where all the bombs and rockets for the day's use were assembled and ready to take to the flight line.

The explosions lasted all day. Thousands of items were thrown as much as a mile away with unexploded ordnance landing all over the base.

The SVN helicopter parking ramp was right next to the exploding area. Several dozen helicopters were destroyed, many already loaded for combat that day.

A friend of mine was in an A-37 squadron there at that time. He was on alert for CAS that morning. The alert facility was a one-room building with a couple of desks and four beds. On each side of it were two aircraft shelters where the four alert A-37s were parked.

They would have been scrambled to attack the launch sites immediately, but there was a problem. The building had only one door and no window. They couldn't push the door open. After trying for several minutes, a voice outside the door yelled for them to stop trying to open the door and take cover. A live Mk-82 had been blown a mile from the explosions and rolled up against the outside of the door.

The guy outside called the command center for help. They stacked the desks and beds near the back wall and laid down against the wall, hoping that the barricade would attenuate an explosion.

After a while, a munitions crew arrived and de-armed the bomb. Then they rolled the bomb away and let the A-37 pilots out.

Heroic Vietnamese A-1 Pilot

My second day in Bien Hoa, I was sitting in Mobile Control beside the runway chatting with the Vietnamese A-37 pilot on duty. We were interrupted by tower telling us that a Vietnamese A-1 Skyraider was inbound with an emergency. The engine had lost all oil pressure. He was 15 miles out on a straight in approach to Bien Hoa.

The A-1 has a huge radial piston engine. It looks like a WW-II fighter.

We grabbed binoculars and looked out the final approach route. We quickly saw an A-1 with a blue smoke trail coming toward us. That had to be it.

At about 10 miles, he was keeping it a bit high in case the engine quit. He was over heavy forest. If it quit, he would have to use the Yankee Extraction system that was installed in the A-1s in Vietnam. This was a rocket that was attached to the top of a parachute mounted behind the pilot. To eject, the pilot could pull a handle that releases his seat belt and fired the rocket after jettisoning the canopy. This pulled the pilot out of his seat by his parachute harness, where he was almost instantly under a fully deployed chute. It worked very well at the low speed of the A-1.

About five miles from the runway, the blue smoke stopped. The other pilot and I looked at each other, both realizing that this meant all oil was gone from the engine. It could seize at any moment. The pilot kept the A-1 well above normal final approach height, aiming for the center of the runway, and put the landing gear down..

Sure enough, about a mile out, the engine seized. The huge 4-blade prop stopped in an X position. With the massive drag from the stopped prop, we didn't think he could reach the runway. There was a large tree line about half a mile from the runway. The A-1 pilot nosed his plane down to gain airspeed and disappeared behind the trees. We thought he was going to crash into the trees.

A few seconds later, it appeared as he zoomed up and over the last of the trees. The runway has a 1,000 foot overrun that is just for safety. He set up a landing attitude and landed hard on all three gear (called a 3-point landing) on the end of the overrun. He bounced, stabilized it again, and made a perfect landing just as he reached the approach end of the runway. He stopped within two plane-lengths right next to our Mobile Control hut.

His outstanding feat of airmanship saved a valuable aircraft and likely avoided injury to himself.

Napalm Release Malfunction

On a daytime CAS mission in southwestern Vietnam, our 2-ship was loaded with 6 Snakeyes on the centerline station and 2 napalm cans on each inboard wing station. We used the Snakeyes first, then hit another target with the napalm. I dropped all 4 napes, but the FAC called "3 splashes."

That was strange. Napalm tanks are ignited by a small piece of white phosphorus. It's in fluid in a small glass bottle. When the tank hits the ground, it rips apart, spreading the gelled gasoline, and breaking the glass bottle. The WP ignites upon contact with air and ignites the nape. There is no way you can get a dud.

I thought I had felt all 4 release, and when Lead checked me over, he said I was "clean", meaning all ordnance was gone.

This was a double turn mission where we would land at Bien Hoa, refuel and rearm, and fly another mission on the way back to Korat. I landed normally at Bien Hoa and taxied off the end of the runway to the de-arm area. The de-arm crew started to walk toward us carrying chocks.

Suddenly, their eyes got really wide and they started franticly drawing their hands across their necks. That's the signal to cut the engines off. Then, they turned and ran.

I quickly shut down both engines, and we climbed out. The de-arm crew stopped and started warily walking toward us pointing under the plane. We turned and looked.

The entire belly of the plane from the leading edge of the wings to the engine nozzles was covered with a layer of napalm (gelled gasoline) about 2 inches thick. It was a creamy white almost the same color as the belly paint. That's why Lead didn't see it while airborne. It was starting to dry and getting very rubbery.

The crew chief said, "It will harden like rock. We'll have to chisel it off and replace some panels if we don't get it off right now. All of us got under the plane and started grabbing large sheets with both hands and peeling it off. We got nearly all of it off.

Unfortunately, once we had it off, we saw significant damage on the plane. There was a 12" long by 6" wide hole where the bottom of the right wing met the fuselage.

The left bomb rack on the right inboard wing station was broken.

The right aft AIM-7 Sparrow Missile (a radar guided air-to-air missile) had the front and rear lower fins ripped off and a hole punched into its warhead. If the warhead had detonated or the napalm had ignited, we would have been lucky if we had time to eject at that low altitude and right in the middle of a battle.

Later analysis by maintenance showed that someone assembling the bomb load had left a half-inch diameter rubber "O" ring out when they installed the bomb rack. The bomb is released by a shotgun shell sized charge firing gas down a tube to release the hooks that hold the bomb lugs.

Without the "O" ring, gas escaped, leaving only enough pressure to open the rear hook fully and the front hook half way. The other 3 nape cans released normally, but when I pulled 5 G's after bomb release, this one pivoted down from the front lug, driving the nose of the can into the bottom of the plane, ripping the front hook out of the bomb rack, and tearing open the napalm can without breaking the glass bottle that would have ignited the nape. Lucky day for us.

Chased a MiG-21

As a new guy First Lieutenant, I flew mostly bombing missions. The more experienced guys flew some air-to-air missions. I did fly a night Combat Air Patrol (CAP) mission protecting B-52's west of Hanoi. At night, all engagements have to be radar. With no visual dogfighting, the young guys can fly these.

These were long missions where we would orbit at the CAP point for half an hour, go to a KC-135 tanker to refuel, then return to the CAP. We would be there 3 or 4 hours if we never got vectored on an intercept. These were my longest missions.

A single MiG-21 came out of China and headed to intercept three B-52's that we were covering. We were vectored to intercept the MiG. Disco (an EC-121 radar plane similar to today's AWACS) identified it as a "Blue Bandit." That was the code word for a MiG-21, our most dangerous adversary.

We got to about 20 miles from him, maybe a minute to missile range, when he turned north toward China and lit his afterburner. A MiG-21 and an F-4E at that altitude could both do about Mach 1.6 in full afterburner. We chased him but couldn't close to missile range before he would get to China. So, we had to pull the power back and head back to the tanker. We had done our job protecting the B-52's.

The last I saw, the 35TFS had 8 confirmed air-to-air kills. Actually, we had 16 stars with crew, weapon, and MiG type painted on our squadron commander's plane when we returned to Korea.

One of them was one of our WSO's, but the F-4E and pilot were from a Korat squadron. Also, one kill was scored by Intel as being hit by missiles from two of our planes. That was even though Intel said that a 4-ship took off, but only one landed.

Another was called an SA-2 shootdown by intel. Our guy fired an AIM-9 (heat seeker) at a MiG-21 up into a clear blue sky with ideal range. However, he then had to dodge an SA-2 SAM.

By the time everyone got back to looking toward the MiG, all they saw was a white parachute, apparently the MiG pilot. Nobody knows for sure which missile hit the MiG.

Two of the others were a pair of MiG-21s that were taxiing in after landing at Yen Bai Airfield. Two of our planes were returning from a Hunter-Killer mission when they looked down and saw them. Lead rolled inverted, pulled into a vertical dive, and emptied the F-4E's 600 rounds of 20mm into them. Both blew up. Six others were also hit on the ground at various times.

B-52 Bomber Escort

I had one night B-52 escort mission. We were to join up with a B-52 over the coast south of the DMZ and escort him to wherever he was going. We found him easily and set up with each of us a few hundred feet out to each side and a bit behind him.

He kept a couple of upper lights on so we could see him. We turned all our lights off. He moved about five miles inland and headed north. We expected him to head for a target, bomb it, and turn offshore.

However, he just kept going up the coast over land. This put us within AAA and SA-2 range all the way.

After several minutes, my Leader couldn't take it anymore, and radioed "Where are we heading?" Someone on the B-52 answered "Didn't they tell you? We're dropping a leaflet bomb every few miles along the coast."

A leaflet bomb was a Cluster Bomb Unit canister filled with paper flyers instead of bomblets. We did this crazy run all the way from the DMZ through Route Packs 1,2,3, and 4. Amazingly, we saw no defensive fire the whole 20 minutes. We couldn't see the bombs as the B-52 dropped them due to darkness.

Lightning

Of course, thunderstorms are almost a daily occurrence in Southeast Asia. One day, we were returning to Korat after a 2-ship CAS mission in SVN. We were winding between thunderstorms. About 50 miles from Korat, the GCA controller split us up for single-ship approaches.

Lead angled left, and I continued straight. We were less than half a mile apart when a huge lightning bolt came from above and behind lead. It split into several separate streaks that surrounded lead's plane, came back together in front of it, and went on to the ground.

I hit the mike button and said, "Lead. Are you okay?"

He answered, "Yes. Why?"

I said, "Didn't that lightning hit you?"

He said, "What lightning?"

Rather than try to explain at that point, I said, "I'll tell you on the ground."

When we got on the ground, my WSO and I told him what we had seen. He said that all they saw was a blinding flash and didn't see a streak. There was no damage to his plane.

LINEBACKER Missions

These missions would put close to 500 aircraft into the air. Several dozen would be tankers, others would be airborne radar warning EC-121's, EB-66 jammers, and other support aircraft with 300 or more fighters. The aircraft would come from all bases in the area and several aircraft carriers.

Most would be F-4's for bombing with other F-4's protecting from MiGs. F-105G Wild Weasels would attack and suppress the anti-aircraft defenses. This would include Hunter-Killer flights. Lead and 2 in those flight would be F-105G Wild Weasels with 3 and 4 being F-4E's with CBUs to hit SAM sites found by the Weasels plus missiles and a gun for air-to-air combat.

All Hunter-Killer missions were flown by our most experienced crews, so I never flew one of those.

All aircrews at each base would have a mass briefing well before dawn. Then, each flight would have their internal briefing.

Fighters would fly as 4-ship flights, but each flight would launch with a spare. The spare would refuel with everyone else. Before departing the tanker, the spare would replace any aircraft that had a mechanical problem.

At the planned time, the four-ship flights would head for the Initial Point to start the target run-in while the spare or the aircraft it replaced would return to base.

During the refueling part of this, the sight of all the aircraft was absolutely amazing. The tankers would fly in echelon formations of seven KC-135's. You could scan all around and see echelons of seven tankers with four or five fighters behind each tanker stretching from horizon to horizon. Of course, I could only see those over Thailand. There would be another huge group over the water to the east.

At the designated time, each flight would head for its target. Meanwhile, the NVN Air Force plus some Chinese and Russian help would prepare to meet the attack. There would be 30 or so MiG fighters, several SA-2 SAM sites, and thousands of AAA guns ready to meet us.

Radios would get busy quickly as the EC-121, call sign Disco, would call out MiGs and many flights called out SAM warnings. Our tactics seemed to work since we would only lose an aircraft about every other day. Each downed crew resulted in a huge recovery effort by Search and Recovery (SAR) forces and some of the LINEBACKER aircraft refueling and returning to cover the SAR.

Korat Dumb Bombers Do the Job

I was assigned to a LINEBACKER mission to hit an installation a few miles west of Hanoi a mile east of where the Black River joins with the Red River. It was 23 60-foot long tin roof buildings that were partly training camp and partly explosives storage. The weather was not good with nearly a full low overcast. Therefore, the mission was planned for a medium altitude level bomb drop in formation. I don't remember the altitude we used, but it was probably about 18,000 feet.

Long Range Navigation (LORAN) transmitters had been placed around the Vietnam area to provide navigation within 200 feet. A LORAN equipped F-4 from Ubon AB would lead. It could navigate precisely enough to do the drop. Two 4-ship flights from Ubon plus our 4-ship would fly together with the only LORAN equipped aircraft leading. The Lead WSO would call the bomb release over the radio. That would send 144 MK-82's raining onto the base.

We were shocked while we were still on the tanker and heard the LORAN leader call at the Initial Point (IP). The two Ubon flights had left the tanker five minutes early!

We immediately headed for the IP. We pushed our speed up. but had no chance of closing a 5-minute gap. That turned out to be fortunate for us. The eight Ubon aircraft arrived over the target area and we heard the most unusual radio call I ever heard. The Lead WSO said, "Ready. Ready. Pickle Pickle Pickle ...... Aww Shit."

All eight of them dropped on his pickle call. Then he noticed that he had forgotten to switch his navigation system from the river intersection that he used to navigate to the actual target coordinates. That put 96 bombs into the river with a few hitting the village next to the river.

We were still over three minutes behind. We were fortunate, because the Ubon flights were busy dodging SAMs immediately after the target run and dodging MiGs on the way out of the country. They attracted the full attention of the air defenses, so our Korat flight never got shot at as far as we know.

Without the LORAN, we had no way of making the level drop. We would have to dive bomb or go home with our bombs. We passed over the target and started a left turn instead of the planned right turn to the egress route. Lead called over the radio that the clouds look thin, so we're going to do a left circle around the target to try to see it.

The rest of us all thought "We're going to do WHAT in the middle of Route Pack 6?" I understand that there were some crude comments between crew members in some aircraft. Meanwhile, the air defenses were still concentrating on the Ubon flights.

As we finished the circle, Lead said "We're going around again. There's a hole in the clouds." As we finished our second circle, the hole drifted over the target area and there were the buildings, just like the SR-71 photo.

We immediately did a 4-ship formation 45 degree dive bomb pass while maintaining pod formation to keep our radar jamming pods effective. (That's an exciting maneuver in itself.) It was south to north, so it was the opposite direction of our planned egress. Our aim was perfect.

All of the buildings disappeared in the explosions of the 48 Mk-82 bombs followed by secondary explosions and large fires. My WSO on that flight, Ray, always carried a very good camera, and Lead knew it. When we pulled out of the pass, Lead said, "Ray. We're going around again so you can take pictures." Thinking this was a crazy idea, we all followed and Ray got the photos. One is shown below. The black smoke is from the bomb explosions. The gray smoke is from structure fires. The white one on the right is a cloud. Since we circled the area half way before taking the photos, the smoke has drifted a bit left to right.

Post-strike photos taken by an RF-4 showed that 21 of the 23 buildings were destroyed and one severely damaged. Only one was intact. Significantly, our precision dive bomb attack hit only the intended target, leaving the nearby village untouched. The 16 ship level attack would have hit a much larger area.

The Korat Wing Commander had that RF-4 photo framed. He and our squadron commander signed it and wrote "Courtesy of the Korat Dumb Bombers", and sent it to the Ubon Wing Commander. All of us in the Korat flight got single-mission Air Medals for this mission.

Smart Bombs

While I was at Korat, the AF introduced the first laser-guided bombs into operation. All of them went to Ubon AB along with the laser designators and training to use them.

One day I was #2 in a 2-ship flight each carrying 12 MK-82 "dumb bombs" as usual. We were assigned to work with a Wolf FAC. The FAC had a target for us near the coast in RP2.

There had been heavy rain that washed a temporary bridge across a small river away. To move supply vehicles south, they were using four barges that could each carry one large truck. The barges were all along the north shore of the river spaced about 100 feet apart. That is a tough target for our weapons load, since we would have to stay high to avoid several AAA guns. Also, it would take a very close hit to damage the barges.

Just after the FAC briefed us on the target, a 2-ship of F-4s from Ubon checked in. Each was carrying two MK-82 bombs with laser guidance systems. The FAC decided to try these new weapons on the barges, since they should have a better chance of success.

The trick with these early systems was that the laser designator was a small laser attached to a small telescope and mounted on a pivot attached to the left canopy rail in the back seat. The pilot would fly a counterclockwise circle around the target, and the WSO would look through the telescope to manually aim the laser at the target.

Another aircraft would then drop the bomb aiming near the target so that it would guide on the laser spot. Obviously, this would not be viable in a highly defended area, but it would be okay for this target.

The Ubon crew worked along the river and scored direct hits on all four barges with no misses. We were fascinated to watch it. The FAC then called us and said "Don't worry. I have another target up the coast a little."

Wolf Down

While at F-4 training at George AFB, I became friends with Rick. He was an F-4 WSO who was stationed at Ubon while I was at Korat. He became a WSO on a Wolf FAC crew. The Air Force used what we called "Fast FACs" to find targets of opportunity in North Vietnam. In the early years, they flew the F-100, but by 1972, they flew the F-4. Daytime their call sign was "Wolf" and nighttime it was "Owl." I worked with them a few times.

On October 5, 1972, I was returning from a night mission when a huge thunderstorm parked right over Korat. We had to divert to Ubon AB and spend the rest of the night there.

Late the next morning, I went to the Officer's Club to get a very late breakfast. While sitting there, Rick walked in. He had just finished eating and had to go to a mission briefing, so we decided to meet at a certain table in the bar at 1700. He headed out the door, waved, and the last thing he said to me was, "I'll buy you a drink when I get back."

I showed up just before 1700 and waited about 15 minutes. Then a couple of Ubon F-4 crews sat down at the next table. They started talking about a missing Wolf. They said that the Wolf was over the

71

Route Pack Two area, but contact was lost. He never came out of NVN.

I asked who the crew was and found out the WSO was Rick. Many of us waited around to hear any more information, but there was no report of a radio call and no emergency beepers.

Other F-4s tried to contact them on their radios, but there was no answer. The weather was a ceiling at 5,000', and no one else was in the area to see any explosion or fire. It was a sad evening waiting around. The next day, we all had to get back to flying our own missions.

Several months later, when the peace treaty was signed in 1973. Rick and his pilot were on the POW list that was provided by the NVN delegation! They were on one of the last planes bringing POWs home.

Two years later, I was at Bergstrom AFB flying O-2s. One evening I was in the Officer's Club shooting pool. (I did that a lot.) I looked up and saw Rick walk into the bar! I headed towards him, but he saw me and yelled across the room, "Banks! I owe you a drink!" I yelled back, "The Hell you do! I'm buying YOU a drink!" We then spent a few hours catching up.

They had been looking for targets in RP 2 under that 5,000' ceiling when they were hit hard. They don't know what hit them, but the aircraft exploded and came apart. They ejected with no time for a radio call. They were so low that they were only in their chutes for a few seconds. They landed right among a group of NVN soldiers and were captured immediately.

They were taken to a concrete bunker along a road near the coast. Rick told me that the area was getting bombed a lot. One attack was so close that the guard at the bunker door was wounded by shrapnel. There was so much bombing along the road that they were never moved from the bunker until after the cease fire. Then, a truck took them to Hanoi to join the rest of the POWs.

After getting back to the States and recovering from the lack of care and food, he was assigned to pilot training. After getting his pilot wings, he was assigned to O-2s at Bergstrom. We were again in the same squadron.

Bad Luck Ejection

I remembered a weird accident that happened in '72. The pilot was a Major who was the senior student in my F-4 class at George AFB.

72

When returning from Vietnam the 300 NM to base, (Saigon, DaNang, and Hanoi are all about 300NM from Korat.) we would often climb to 30,000' or so over Vietnam and start a gradual descent while still over Laos. We would leave the power at cruise or higher setting. Normally, that would give us about Mach 1.1 or 1.2 all the way until slowing down for the pattern at Korat. That would get the plane back to maintenance 5 or 10 minutes early to help turn it for another sortie.

The Major was doing that returning to his home base, Ubon AB. However, he had a hung Mk-82 on an inboard station. The plane started a pitch oscillation that quickly went divergent. The WSO thought the plane was about to come apart and initiated a sequenced ejection while nearly supersonic.

They were well above the 500-knot max speed for the ejection seat. The WSO didn't call the ejection, so the Major was still trying to fly the plane. The WSO received several injuries from flailing limbs. The Major's left arm hit the cockpit side since his hand was still on the throttles and was broken in several places. His right arm and one leg were broken by flailing in the high speed wind blast.

When he landed, he ended up lying with his good leg between two tree stumps that were only a couple of feet apart. Due to the broken arms and leg, he couldn't remove his chute harness or move anywhere. After a few minutes, a Jolly Green showed up to pick them up. The Jolly landed right next to the Major. The rotor downwash inflated the chute which pulled him sideways, breaking the good leg between the stumps.

It was calculated later that, at that transonic speed, the single bomb caused turbulent flow over the slab, causing a divergent pitch oscillation.

Meteorite

After taking off for a night mission, my flight was refueling from a KC-135 over northeast Thailand. We were heading north when a bright light trailing sparks appeared at our 10 o'clock position moving fast right to left and angling down.

The boomer in the tanker started yelling "*Sam! Sam! Breakaway! Breakaway!*" Breakaway means to disconnect immediately and move away from the refueling boom. He disconnected and retracted the boom. My flight Lead calmly said, "SAMS usually come from the ground up. That was probably a meteorite." The boomer quietly cleared Lead back into contact position.

73

Jane Fonda Visit

There are many reasons that Vietnam veterans often say "I'm not Fond'a Jane." This pun was irresistible. Her traitorous actions outraged those of us who were putting our lives on the line. She apparently wanted the Communists to win, and was quite willing to do anything to make us look bad and the NVN government good.

One of the incidents during her visit that still has me seething was particularly personal. She appeared standing in front of a building that had a sign over the entrance showing that it had once been a French school. It clearly showed bomb and fire damage. There were also burned areas around the building and trees that had been blown down by bombs. She posed there and told reporters that the day before, "American Imperialist pilots" had bombed this school, killing many children and teachers. This photo was on the cover of newspapers around the world.

I immediately recognized the building, since I was one of those pilots who bombed it the day before. That day, a Wolf FAC in an F-4 spotted a number of ammo trucks parked in the trees around this school. The school had been abandoned since the French pulled out years earlier. It was sometimes used as a stopover for convoys moving south. It had been bombed before.

We attacked the trucks with MK-82 bombs, destroying several of them and some trees and leaving large fires burning. We also hit the building, since that is where the truck crews probably were. Apparently they cleared the trucks and bodies away before taking Fonda there.

Fonda believed every lie told to her by the North Vietnamese. No one would tell us where she was staying in Hanoi. That was a good thing, because it would have probably caused a multi-aircraft midair collision as everyone "accidentally" missed their targets on the next LINEBACKER mission.

End of Tour Mission

My last mission was a night CAP. We had an orbit point just inside of Laos from NVN. We protected three B-52 missions, going to a tanker to top off after each. No MiGs came up that night. After about four hours, we headed back to Korat.

As we approached Korat, the radar controller told us that Korat was closed due to a thunderstorm. We had to divert to Ubon AB. That was about 100 miles behind us, so we headed back there. By the time we landed, we had been airborne nearly five hours. Most of that time had been above 30,000 feet altitude.

At high altitude, the cockpit oxygen system provides nearly pure oxygen to the mask. Pure oxygen absorbs into the inner ear tissue faster than normal air. I didn't know that I had a slight infection in my left ear which, during this flight, partially blocked normal air flow out of my inner ear. Therefore, after landing, the pressure in my inner ear kept getting lower and lower for the next few hours.

Uban didn't have any open beds for us, so we had to go to a hotel in the town for the rest of the night. About 0400, I woke with a terrible pain in my left ear. It was the worst ear block I had ever felt by far. Nothing I tried would clear it. I had to call for a base taxi to pick me up and get me to the base hospital emergency room.

At the hospital, the on duty Flight Surgeon took one look into my ear and said, "You have a raging infection in that ear!" By then, the pain was terrible, and my ear drum was bulging in, so he gave me some strong antibiotic for the infection and a Darvon II for the pain. He had me lay down in a small emergency room with only a bed and a small table. He said he would check back shortly.

When he did, the pain was only worse. He decided that I needed more powerful pain relief. He had to call the standby pharmacy Sergeant to open the drug safe. When the Sergeant arrived, he pulled a Codeine pill out. It was spherical about the size of a standard marble. I managed to swallow it. Then, the doc told me to lay back down in that same room for a while.

I did, and the pain slowly subsided. After several minutes, the phone on the table rang, and I answered it. It was the doctor asking how I was. I told him the pain was decreasing.

After I hung up the phone, a cat walked into the room. It came to the bed and jumped on. I scratched its head and petted it a little. Then it jumped off and left.

A few minutes later, the doctor walked into the room and asked how I was doing. I said, "I just told you on the phone." As I said that, I pointed to the table where there was *no phone*! Apparently, there was no cat either. The combination of Darvon II and Codeine caused hallucinations. I still remember those events today as if they were totally real.

After this experience, I swore to never touch nor let a member of my family touch a hallucinogenic drug again. They implant seemingly real, but totally false memories.

There was a story going around Korat about a serious incident involving hallucinogenic drugs. It seems that an F-4 pilot from a Korat squadron took off on a standard mission carrying 12 MK-82 bombs.

On the way across Thailand, he armed the weapons and rolled in on a Thai village. His WSO asked what he was doing. When there wasn't an answer, the WSO thought fast and pulled the circuit breakers for the bomb system. That kept him from dropping the bombs.

After a lot of talking and yelling, the WSO got the pilot to agree to fly back to Korat and land. Then, on final approach, the pilot started trying to push the stick forward and dive into the ground. The WSO fought him for control and got him to complete the landing. Luckily, the Air Force had added rear cockpit flight controls that the Navy didn't feel was necessary. The WSO had called ahead on the radio, so an ambulance met them as they stopped on the runway.

I heard later that, while he was in college, the pilot was at a party where someone put LSD on a bowl of potato chips. Several people ate them and the pilot had an especially bad "trip." Flashbacks can happen at any time, especially in a stressful situation. This was probably what happened. Unfortunately, that probably ended his flying career.

Departure Crash #4

We returned to Kunsan in October 1972. I flew a total of 38 combat missions. Several others turned back due to weather or mechanical problems or were just training.

We were replaced by the A-7 squadron that the top graduate from my pilot training class went to. They could fly the same close air support missions that we did in the F-4, but they didn't need to refuel enroute like we did. They also had the first computer-aided visual bombing system, so they were usually much more accurate than an F-4. This made them very valuable for CAS.

One day over Cambodia, shortly after the A-7s replaced us at Korat, his A-7 had a large oil leak that quickly drained all the oil from the engine. Unlike the F-4, the A-7 has only one engine. They never found out for sure, but he may have taken a small arms hit during a low attack.

The closest place to land was the airport at Phenom Penh, the capital of Cambodia. He headed there, lined up for the runway, and prepared to land.

About three miles from landing, the engine seized. That shut down all hydraulics and froze the flight controls. His only option was to eject.

The plane crashed into a hospital, killing a few people including doctors. He landed on the tile roof of a 2-story building and rolled off as the chute collapsed. He fell two stories. The fall broke several bones and caused internal injuries. He survived, but would never fly again.

Rick Keyt's Website

Here is a website by Rick Keyt. He was a WSO in my squadron while we were at Korat. It includes many stories and photos about our time at Korat. Yes, all are totally true. Many more aren't written down. The site is a tribute to our time in combat.

http://www.keytlaw.com/f-4/category/air-war-links/

Fate of Korat AB

After the Vietnam War ended, Korat AB was enlarged into a modern airport shared by the Thai Air Force and a civilian terminal. During the 1990's a new Nakhon Ratchasima civilian airport was constructed a few miles to the east, and Korat again became a Royal Thai Air Base.

Kunsan Air Base, South Korea

https://www.kunsan.af.mil/
October 1972

B ack at Kunsan, I finally started living in my assigned barracks room. For the next five months, I flew many missions around Korea and Japan. Twice I delivered aircraft to the F-4 depot maintenance facility at Ching Chuan Kang Air Base, Taiwan (CCK) and picked up finished ones. I also sat several days of alert duty at Kunsan.

First and Last Kimchi

A few days after returning to Kunsan from Korat, several of the squadron guys decided to go to a restaurant in Kunsan City that they had enjoyed before deploying. There was room for 12, so I went along to experience something in Korea off base. Up to that point, I had never been off base at Kunsan.

This was a traditional Korean formal restaurant that was often attended by businessmen in the area. It was for men only, as many things were in Korea. There was a square table less than a foot from the floor that had three seat cushions next to each side. A young lady in traditional brightly colored dresses was assigned to each of us. The 12 ladies set small burners on the table, brought in food, and cooked it as we all sat there talking.

When the food was ready, the ladies put plates in front of us and put servings of various food on them. The food was slightly spicier than I prefer, but it was all good. There were three kinds of meat, three or four vegetables, rice, and kimchi. Of course, I didn't know what any of it was called.

Kimchi is a traditional Korean stable eaten at most meals. It is made by mixing chopped cabbage with several powerful spices, putting it into ceramic pots, and burying it for a few months to ferment. When needed for food, they dig up a pot, cook the kimchi, and serve it.

While they were serving, I noticed that we had no eating utensils, not even chopsticks. After the food was served, each young lady pulled out chopsticks and started feeding us. It seems that the normal procedure was that the men would sit and discuss things while paying no attention at all to the ladies. It was just part of the service. They would put another bite in our mouths any time we stopped talking.

After enjoying several bites of various things and getting into the idea of ignoring that I was being fed, the inevitable happened. My server put a large bite of kimchi into my mouth. PAIN! BURNING PAIN! Surely she had aimed a blowtorch into my mouth. I yelled and

78

spit it into my hand. That didn't help much. Lots of whatever was available to drink finally got me breathing again. Everybody laughed, because they knew how spicy it was.

I have never touched kimchi since and never will.

Emergency at Kadena

Kadena Air Base, Okinawa, was a refueling stop between Korea and Taiwan. An F-4D straight out of major maintenance could have unexpected problems. On one of my trips returning a plane from CCK to Kunsan, I took off from Kadena, headed north, and climbed to a cruise altitude above 30,000'. The flight route passes over southern Japan to Korea.

Shortly after settling into cruise, I discovered that I couldn't transmit on the radio. We couldn't fly into Japanese airspace with no radio contact, so we decided to return to Kadena. We set the transponder to the comm out code of 7600 and turned back.

We planned to follow standard instrument flight routes to a TACAN non-precision approach with a transition to visual for landing. We also dumped part of our fuel to get below maximum safe landing weight. Air Traffic Control saw us returning and had me squawk Ident on the radar transponder to confirm. That shows ATC a code on their radar confirming that we heard him. He then cleared us for the approach and passed the current weather.

To our amazement, the weather had quickly turned bad. The ceiling and visibility were at visual minimums. As we approached the airfield, a plane taking off had a problem, had to abort takeoff, and couldn't clear the runway in time for us to land, so we had to go around.

When I raised the gear and flaps, I got a red BLC warning light. The F-4D has a boundary layer control (BLC) system that allows you to fly slower for landing by blowing air at high speed across the top of the wing. The Navy needed that for carrier landings.

It sends hot, high-pressure air from the engine to tiny holes on the top of the wing leading edge when the flaps are down. The leading edge flaps cover the holes when up. If they are up with BLC operating, it will start a fire in the wing. Thus, the red warning light.

The immediate emergency procedure is to lower the gear and flaps and leave them down. I did so, then declared an emergency and changed the squawk to 7700, the emergency code.

This go-around caused us to have to fly a 10-mile long left rectangle to get back to the instrument approach at low altitude with gear and flaps down, causing us to use a high power setting. We only had enough fuel to try this twice.

The weather kept getting worse. About 10 miles out from the runway, we were in heavy rain, dark clouds, and strong wind gusts. Then, the radio quit receiving.

All I could do was keep heading for the TACAN station, keep clear of the water using the radar altimeter, and hope we would see the runway. It worked. I spotted the runway almost dead ahead and got it on the ground in one piece.

Now, the plane had to be fixed. The repairs required running an engine at various times to find the problem, fix it, and test it.

The Kadena wing had F-4Cs. However, the maintenance crews were not certified to run the engine on a D. I had to stay at Base Ops all day for three days to run the engine each time they needed it. At least it gave me time for three Kobe steaks and Mai Tai's at Sam's Anchor Inn, a great Japanese restaurant a short distance from Kadena. That cost only $5 for the steak and $1 for the drink.

Radio Controlled Model Plane

During my off-duty time at Kunsan, I built a radio-controlled (RC) plane. It had a 5-foot wingspan with operating flaps, elevator, ailerons, rudder, and throttle. It had a high, straight wing and enough power to do all the standard aerobatic maneuvers.

With the flaps down, I could fly it slow enough to hover into a light breeze. Part of a paved ramp away from the flight line was reserved for RC flying on weekends. A Major in my squadron was highly experienced and taught me to fly the RC plane. The trick is to project your mind into the plane's point of view. It takes practice to keep in sync with left and right in relation to the plane.

While learning to fly the traffic pattern and land, I crashed it into a hangar roof. I gave a maintenance guy a case of beer to climb up and get it for me. It was easily reparable. I flew this plane for years and only crashed it this one time. I guess this makes me an early Air Force Remotely Piloted Aircraft (RPV) pilot.

Today, the news media has converted this to "Drone Pilot." They refuse to understand that the term "drone" actually means an unmanned vehicle that can fly and navigate on its own. A drone doesn't need a pilot except for takeoff, landing, and taxiing.

Chased a MiG Again

One day while on air defense alert, the bell rang and the four of us jumped in the truck heading for our two F-4Ds that were each armed to the teeth with four Sparrows, two Sidewinders, and a 20mm gun pod. After takeoff, we expected to get the usual radio call telling us it was an exercise and that we would be doing a training intercept.

However, this time, the order was a vector to the north with the words "Your signal is BUSTER." That meant to stay in full afterburner and make the intercept ASAP even if there wasn't enough fuel to get back.

Four MiG-21's in a tactical formation at low level had crossed the DMZ heading straight south. We were halfway there with missiles armed before the intercept was called off. The MiG pilots had missed a turn point on a training mission and turned back north when they realized their mistake.

We returned to re-cock the planes on alert, but it took quite a while for the adrenalin to wear off and our fangs to retract. We figured that the instructor leading that flight was shot the same day. That would be normal North Korean procedure.

Comedy Scramble

There was another interesting air defense scramble that I witnessed. I was at the alert aircraft shelters at the south end of the runway preflighting an F-4D to go on alert for the next 24 hours. I was setting up the cockpit, so I had my helmet on and the radio on the scramble frequency.

It was common to end an alert tour with a practice scramble. The pilots of the crews about to go off of alert were Mike and Larry.

Mike was flight lead. They had a running contest on who could do things better. On alert, this included getting airborne quicker. The requirement was five minutes from the bell to airborne. Usually it would take from 4 to 4 ½ minutes.

Whoever gets on the runway first is Lead until the assigned Lead catches up, if he can. Usually, the two aircraft pull out of the shelters at nearly the same time, so the wingman lets the assigned leader go ahead.

My pair was about finished cocking our aircraft, but still had power on and radios on.

The aircraft on alert have to be full of fuel, so there is always a few cups of fuel that run out the overflow vents as the day warms up. The overflow vents are pipes half-way out the trailing edge of each wing between the flap and the aileron.

To catch this fuel, there is a red metal garbage can that sits under each vent. To avoid sparks, there is a braided steel grounding wire attached to the can with a plug on the other end that plugs into a receptacle on the bottom of the wing. Part of the scramble procedure is for the crew chief to unplug those wires after engine start.

Sure enough, the scramble bell went off just before we changed who was on duty. Mike and Larry were already standing near the aircraft and were starting engines within a minute. They were ready within three minutes, and started to head for the runway. Larry eased off to let Mike lead.

Mike's crew chief forgot the plug on the right side. When Mike pulled out of the alert shelter, the can was bouncing along behind his right wing, still attached. Within seconds, he was pulling onto the runway while accelerating for takeoff.

Larry started yelling, "Lead! You're dragging your can! You're dragging your can!"

Of course, due to their competitive spirit, Mike misinterpreted this as being chided by Larry for being too slow. He pushed the power up and headed down the runway.

Larry called again, but Mike was nearly airborne by then. Larry stopped on the runway, because he thought the can might break loose and get in front of him.

Just as Mike lifted the nose to take off, the cable broke at the wing connection and the can bounced off the right side of the runway with the cable attached. Larry saw that the runway was clear, so he pushed the power to max and took off. The delay put him a couple of miles behind Mike.

The scramble was cancelled after about five minutes. Larry joined up with Mike, told him about the overflow can, and looked over the area where the can attached and the tail area on that side. He couldn't see any damage, so they continued the flight to fly practice intercepts on each other. The only damage was a cable that broke off right at the plug and a banged up catch can.

Later that week, there was a suggestion passed to all the aircrews that we might try to be a little more explicit with our radio calls.

Departure Crash #5 (My F-4 Tried to Kill Me)

Crashed + Burned   Lt. Banks (pilot)

1.15 hours   March 23, 1973   Lt. Price   (Navigator)

Kunsan AFB Korea

The is a photo of F-4D 650728 about to catch the approach end barrier at Kunsan AB. This barrier is used in emergencies where control or stopping after landing might be a problem. It is only possible due to the Navy tailhook. Each week, one sortie at Kunsan was selected to do an engagement at the end of their mission. This was for barrier testing and training of the barrier crew. It also provided a practice engagement for pilots. I was never selected for one. This photo was given to me by the barrier crew member who took it about a week before the flight described here.

On March 23, 1973, my last F-4 flight, which was in 728 at Kunsan, lasted about 15 seconds; 17 seconds if you add the parachute time. We were having our first Operational Readiness Inspection (ORI) after spending April through October 1972 flying combat over Vietnam. It was a 5-day test where we had to prove we were ready to handle our defense of South Korea mission.

The early days included air intercepts of various incoming aircraft, demonstrating all the types of weapons deliveries the F-4D could do at Koo Ni Range, and air-to-air refueling. We also had to do live bomb drops on Nightmare Range up north near the Korean DMZ. Since most of us had just finished several months of actual combat, the ORI was going very well.

On the last day of the ORI, we had to do a mass launch of two squadrons of aircraft plus any extras we could generate. Each aircraft had its own separate mission, but all started by flying the same low-level route to Koon Ni Range.

I was not on the flying schedule for that day, but I was given the last of the extra aircraft, tail number 65-0728, and assigned the call sign Deben 92. It was great to not be left out of the big day.

My WSO was Ron, my usual crewmate. We were loaded with both wing drop tanks and the huge (600 gal) centerline tank for a maximum range mission. On the left inboard wing station, we had a 2,500 pound inert practice bomb.

Takeoff would be to the south where the Yellow Sea starts right at the end of the runway. The route wound through South Korea ending at Koon Ni Range on the west coast well north of Kunsan.

All 40 or so aircraft were cocked to 5-minute alert status and we sat in the cockpits waiting for the scramble signal. While waiting, it's impossible to not continue going through all checks on switch positions, instrument settings, and navigation systems to be sure everything would go well. We wanted this to go perfectly.

When we were scrambled, we were about halfway down the takeoff list. We got the signal, cranked the engines, and headed for the runway. Due to being heavy, the takeoff role would be longer than usual on the bumpy runway with a shallow climb after takeoff.

The takeoff role was normal. After the long roll, we reached rotation speed, and I lifted the nose 10 degrees. Liftoff was at the calculated speed, and I raised the landing gear and flaps.

Just as the indicators said "UP", there was a jolt and a sound like a muffled explosion. Immediately, the left engine fire light illuminated. Fire lights indicate a fire around an engine. Overheat lights indicate fire around the afterburner section of an engine. We had just passed the end of the runway and were now over water.

On tower radio frequency, I said: "Deben 92 has a fire light." Then, I reached for the button to jettison the external load, intending to shut off the left engine next.

Before my hand reached the button, the right fire light, both overheat lights, and most of the caution light panel also lit up. At the same time, I realized that the aircraft was pitching up and rolling left even though I had the stick full forward and right. I made the decision to bail out and noticed that both engines were winding down just before I yanked the throttles to cutoff. I had the idea of cutting off the fuel flow to the fire until we ejected – not really necessary, and wasted one second.

84

According to witnesses, much of the aircraft was engulfed, and the flames trailed twice the length of the aircraft. Ron said later that he looked left and right and the inboard half of both wings was on fire. In the forward cockpit, I never actually saw the fire. All the bad warning lights that you hope to never see were illuminated, and the flight controls quit working. "Speed is Life" and we were out of it!

I ordered "Bailout, Bailout, Bailout", and Ron wasn't there for the last two.

We ejected very low out of control, rolling left, and descending. Ron's seat fired at about 600 feet over the water and mine about 200 feet. There is a 1.5 second delay between them to get the WSO clear. That delay was more than a lifetime for several F-4 pilots.

The canopy jettisons first.

Then the Martin Baker seat fires a ballistic charge that kicks the seat out of the cockpit sliding up a rail.

Six feet up the rail, a lanyard triggers a rocket that fires for a couple of seconds. You experience 17 G's momentarily as you clear the vertical tail.

I was holding full right rudder in an attempt to remain upright until ejecting. If you sit upright and push out with one foot, your back bows out from the seat. This is *not* the optimum position for ejection.

Then, a small pilot parachute opens, stabilizing you feet down still in the seat.

Then, the main chute opens followed by the seatbelt being released.

Next, a strap (the "butt-kicker") that runs from the top of the seat to the front tightens up, kicking you out of the seat with a fully deployed chute.

All worked as designed. *Thank you Martin Baker!*

Due to the rolling and sinking, I went straight horizontal at about 200 feet.

When I was free of the seat and under the chute, I immediately pulled the cords to inflate my life preserver unit (LPU) and disconnected my oxygen mask from my helmet so that I wouldn't inhale water.

I hit the water two seconds after my chute opened.

This whole sequence took probably five seconds. My visual memory of it is just a big blur. One more second in the aircraft and I wouldn't have made it.

All my excellent water survival training was running through my head. I even remembered that we had been told about a cold water test the Air Force had done. They had several people jump at the same time into a pool that had been cooled with huge ice blocks to about 40 degrees, and told them to come out when they couldn't stand it any longer.

All were briefed on what was going to happen and each was asked how they thought they would do and how they are preparing mentally. About half of them said they would brace themselves and tough it out. The rest said they just think, "This is going to be *really* cold!"

The ones playing tough were the first ones to come out.

I thought "This is going to be *really* cold!"

My chute stayed inflated and was dragging me mostly under water.

As trained at Homestead, I spread my legs to stabilize, rolled onto my back, and tried to jettison the chute. However, at water entry, my right glove had rolled up over my fingers, so I couldn't get to the tiny flat bar that releases the chute harness.

Still mostly under water, I reached my right hand up the harness as high as I could to pull myself up the riser to where I could use my left hand to release the latch.

That worked. I was free from the chute.

That didn't help much, because I then found that I couldn't breathe! I couldn't inhale or exhale. I struggled, but my chest was paralyzed. I realized that I was about to pass out and I remember thinking, "It's a shame to make it this far and die."

Right after that, I think I passed out. The next thing I knew, just a few seconds later I think, I was taking deep breaths. The doctors explained this to me later. They said that the shock of the cold water caused my breathing muscles to spasm, all contracting at the same time. The act of passing out caused them to relax, instantly restarting my breathing. It's a good thing that I had inflated my LPU to kept my head out of the water and pulled the oxygen mask off.

Cold!!! Numbing cold! The water was 45F with air temp 42F and about a 20-knot wind blowing onshore. I tried to climb into my one-man raft that had inflated automatically.

It was an old orange raft just like the one I used in water survival training. It was scheduled to be replaced within a month. It didn't completely inflate. Also, the oral inflation tube was bent, and couldn't be used.

It took me several minutes to get into the raft. When I was in it, I was still in the water from the waist down, and from the waist up, I was exposed to the cold wind in my soaked flight suit and jacket.

Since this was an ORI, we were wearing full combat gear except for the pistol. That included the survival vest with two radios, two flares, and other useful items. I pulled out one of the radios, set it on guard frequency, and made a call:

"Mayday! Mayday! Mayday! This is Deben 92 Alpha. I'm in my raft and I'm okay." Of course, I was sure that all leadership had seen this happen, so they knew about the crash.

To my surprise, I was answered by the Wing Commander, Col Paul Kautu. I repeated that I was in my raft and okay and asked if Bravo was okay. Alpha and Bravo refers to the front seater and back seater. Before I could hear an answer, my radio quit. It seemed the battery was dead. The other one didn't work either, and a spare battery didn't work. I think the cold water immersion ruined them. At least I knew that they knew I was alive and in my raft.

I saw nothing but open water around me. I had no idea what rescue might be available or what had happened to Ron. For many years, the Air Force had an HH-43, callsign "Pedro", positioned at each air base on 5-minute alert to react to crashes. Well, the Pedros had only saved two people in over 30 years, so the Air Force decided they weren't cost effective and decommissioned all of them three weeks before this accident. We could have doubled the number of saves.

In Korea, we had two HH-3 Jolly Green Giants on alert at Osan AB. They could get airborne within 15 minutes. Of course, it was also more than a half hour flight to Kunsan from there. According to the charts we used at that time, we would be past the expected survival time of 45 minutes in the cold water by then. The "time of useful consciousness" was 35 minutes. The rafts helped a little.

I found out later that Col Kautu saw the crash and jumped into action. He was in his staff car and noticed an Army Huey sitting in front of Base Operations. He called the Wing Command Post on his radio and told them to have Wing Life Support take 4 LPUs and two pieces of rope at least 15 or 20 feet long to the Huey. He ran into the Base Ops snack bar where the Huey pilots were eating, confirmed that was their Huey outside, and told them to get ready to take off as soon as the LPUs arrived.

Life Support was quick to get the stuff and the pilots started the Huey while waiting. That is why Col Kautu answered my Mayday. He was on the radio in the Huey. He inflated the LPUs and tied two together on the end of each rope with the other ends tied to the Huey. He intended to find us, have the Huey hover over us so that we could get hold of the LPUs, and lift us to shore to get out of the cold water.

It turned out that one of the alert Jollys was being used to get an ORI inspector from Kunsan to Tageau. Kunsan tower called them and had them turn back. It was over the crash site within 25 minutes, before the Huey could find us. I never saw the Huey.

Personally, I think Col Kautu should have received a medal for quick thinking. His makeshift system would probably have saved us if the one Jolly hadn't been nearby.

I was sitting in my raft, huddling from the cold, looking at the column of black smoke where our plane crashed. At that point, two rivers join and flow into the sea, and the 14-foot tide was going out, so I was rapidly being carried out to sea and was already miles away. When the Jolly arrived, I could barely see it as a dot on the horizon. It was circling around the smoke looking for us in the water.

By this time, I was shivering severely, and my fingers were stiff. I used both thumbs to pull the zipper on the flare pocket on my vest open. I got a flare out but couldn't grasp it to fire it. You are supposed to put one thumb through a ring on one end, hold the flare out from you with the other hand, and yank the lanyard.

My fingers were no longer capable of a grip, so I had to clamp it to my chest with one hand and yank the ring with the other. I got it away from my chest without burning myself and got the dense, red smoke billowing.

As soon at the red smoke appeared, the Jolly pivoted toward me and made a high-speed dash to hover right over my head. The PJ was on the Forest Penetrator rescue device and down to me within seconds. He used his huge knife to deflate my raft and cut me away from all the ropes and straps. Then he helped me get onto the forest penetrator. He held me in place, and we rode it up to the Jolly together.

Inside the Jolly, the PJ and the ORI inspector took my boots off, poured the water out the door, and covered me on a cot with several blankets. The ORI inspector said, "We're going over to pick up your buddy, now." That was the first I knew what had happened to him. What a relief! We flew to Ron and picked him up quickly.

We spent about a half hour in the water before being rescued. Ron was okay, but I got two compression fractures due to holding the rudder.

We both came within a few minutes of the "expected survival time," It was lucky that I was picked up first. Ron had a new raft that fully inflated and had a spray shield that you could wrap around you and fasten with Velcro. He could stay slightly warmer.

In both the Jolly and the ambulance, I was shaking violently from hypothermia. I was still in a cold wet flight suit and jacket.

I shuffled to the ambulance and tried to step in. I couldn't raise a foot more than 3 or 4 inches from the ground. The flight surgeon immediately yelled, "Put this man on a stretcher!"

Here I am (wearing my helmet) being put on a stretcher to get into the ambulance. Ron is the guy in a helmet already in the ambulance. I

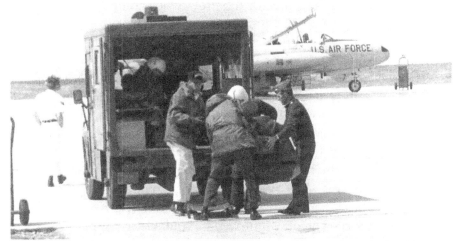

don't know the story on the airman in short sleeve hospital whites on this 42 degree day.

They piled more blankets on top of me. It helped a little. In the Emergency Room, they had to hold me from shaking so they could cut my clothes off. Then, they dried me and piled warm blankets on me.

They tried to take my temperature, but they only had the old mercury thermometers that don't read anything below 94F. It took two hours of warming to reach 94. They estimated that I was down to about 87. At 85, a person usually goes into a coma.

There is always a response to a crash simulation as part of an ORI. That hadn't been done yet, and this was the last day of the ORI. Therefore, the night crew did not go home and all emergency services including the entire hospital, were prepared to react immediately at any time. When the call about a crash went out, they all thought it was an exercise. The fire trucks, ambulances, security police, and supervisor cars immediately headed for the flight line. They saw the smoke and headed for it. Everyone was surprised to see that the column of smoke was a mile off shore. This couldn't be an exercise! The emergency crews did an amazing job throughout this emergency.

The accident investigation had great difficulty, because the plane rolled inverted and went nose first into a sandbar that had a foot of water over it even at low tide. There is a 14-foot tide there and it is the mouth of two rivers. Everything was buried deep in sand within days. The Navy used a barge with a crane for a month to pull out what they could.

They couldn't tell anything from the wreckage. However, they determined that one member of the crew who mounted the centerline fuel tank had finished his training, but his supervisor had not yet signed it off in his records. Therefore, it is possible that he did something wrong. This seems very unlikely.

The next month, back in the States, a similar fire happened in another F-4D, only it was later in the flight. Each of the five months after my accident, another F-4D had a major fuselage fuel leak.

The first four caught fire and the crews ejected, but the last one didn't catch fire. It was very close to base (I think Luke AFB) when the wingman told them that fluid that looks like fuel was pouring out from several panels. The pilot immediately pulled the power back, turned to the base, and landed within a few minutes. He stopped it on the runway ASAP. The crew climbed out quickly as fuel poured out of numerous places, and fire trucks sprayed foam on it.

The investigation quickly found the problem. An F-4D has 6 fuel cells in the fuselage. The largest is number 3 which holds 1,800 pounds of JP4. That one feeds the engines, and all the other tanks feed into it. That means that #3 is nearly full almost all the time.

The tank is a very complex shape made with flat aluminum panels of various shapes welded together to fit as much fuel as possible into the space available. There is a rubber bladder shaped to fit inside the tank. The fuel should stay inside of the bladder.

However, there was a bad batch of #3 tank bladders made. Several F-4D's manufactured at about the same time had the bad bladders. They leaked, letting fuel get against the aluminum welds. Over a few years, this corroded the welds. Eventually a weld would split open, dumping most of 1,800 pounds of JP4 into the engine bays.

Ours apparently split during takeoff roll while heavy weight making a long takeoff roll on a bumpy runway. The fuel flowed back along the belly and ignited when it reached the afterburner plume.

The squadron did not lose an aircraft, even in combat, while I was flying with them except for mine.

Since I was in the last month of my tour at Kunsan, and I was going to be wearing a back brace for three months, I was sent early to my next assignment.

My next aircraft was the O-2. Since it doesn't have an ejection seat, I was put back on flying status in just three months instead of the usual six.

Several years later, I was at a conference and started talking to a couple of rescue helicopter pilots. I offered to buy them drinks and told them I owe my life to guys like them. I told them about my experience in Korea and discovered that one of them was the pilot who flew the hover when I was picked up! Small world.

The only permanent effect of my injury was two compression fractures that changed the shape of my back slightly. It left me 1 ½ inches shorter.

Since the AF allows 5 minutes of taxi time to count in flying time, I logged 0.1 hours for that flight.

Bergstrom AFB, Texas

May 1993

O-2A

702nd Tactical Air Support Squadron (TASS)

https://en.wikipedia.org/wiki/702d_Tactical_Air_Support_Squadron

At the end of my 12-month "remote tour" at Kunsan, over half of which I spent at Korat AB, Thailand, I was assigned to the 702 TASS at Bergstrom AFB. Larry got the same assignment.

The reason that we got these assignments was that US involvement in the Vietnam War had just ended. The F-4 crews from closing squadrons in Thailand were getting the stateside fighter assignments. The fact that we were in Thailand 7 months out of our 12-month tour in Korea was ignored.

At Bergstrom, I was a Forward Air Controller (FAC) flying the O-2. While in Vietnam, I was controlled several times by an O-2 FAC, usually with a callsign of Covey.

The FAC maintains contact with the ground commander in the area and controls fighters to attack enemy forces in close proximity to friendly troops.

We could mark targets using 2.75 inch rockets with White Phosphorus (WP) warheads. The WP (usually referred to as Willie Pete) breaks open upon impact and burns on contact with air, making a small sustained cloud of bright white smoke. This is the same stuff used as a fuse to ignite napalm.

For close air support training for both us and the fighter crews, we would deploy two O-2s for two or three days at a time to fighter bases west of the Mississippi River. We were all assigned to support a specific Army Battalion and worked on the ground with them as the Air Liaison Officer (ALO) and Ground FAC in addition to flying airborne FAC missions.

Training for FACs and ALOs was at the Air/Ground Opertions School (AGOS) at Hurlburt Field, FL. This school taught how to integrate air power into ground combat. The training for flying the O-2 was at Holly Field, like Hurlburt, an auxiliary of Eglin AFB on the Gulf coast.

Arrival Crash #6

Luckily, no one was aboard for this crash. Just before I got to Holly Field, a tornado hit the O-2 flight line. Buildings there consisted of 3 house trailers. One was the flight ops building, one was the maintenance office and shop, and the other was equipment and spare parts storage. The ops trailer was turned onto its side, the maintenance trailer was ripped apart, and the storage trailer was undamaged.

Two O-2's were pushed together with minor damage, but one O-2 was flipped onto its back. It was reparable but took months.

Flying the O-2 is just like any light aircraft and not difficult. The main trick is that AF pilots from fighters had spent pilot training and operational aircraft flying with the right hand on the control stick between our legs and our left hand on the throttles. The O-2 is controlled by the left hand on a control yoke and the right had on the throttles. That took a lot of concentration at first to develop new reflexes. Of course, your reflexes don't have to be so sharp when flying around at 125 knots instead of 500.

Fort Bliss, TX, Field Exercise

One of the first exercises in which I participated on the ground with the Army was at Fort Bliss, TX. This is just northwest of El Paso. Located on Ft Bliss is Biggs Army Air Field (AAF). At that time, Ft Bliss was home to the only division in the US Army that trained in the desert. It was an armored division with primary fighting equipment being the M60 Patton tank and the M113 Armored Personnel Carrier (APC).

A large area north of El Paso is restricted area that is used for Army training. This area is desert with many sand dunes, each with bushes and tumbleweed on the top. From the air it's just spots of green every few hundred feet.

It's not likely that we would use an O-2 to support an armored unit in combat. Enemy armored units have antiaircraft weapons that make it impossible for a low, slow aircraft to operate in the area. Therefore, we expected to work from the ground as an Air Liaison Officer (ALO) located with a forward unit commander.

We worked closely with the artillery units providing fire support. That's a problem when in our jeep. A jeep can't get through rugged or wet terrain like a tracked vehicle. Soft sand is a particular problem. Also, it's not armored at all. Army personnel refer to the jeep as a quarter-ton truck. Usually, they just say "quarter-ton." Army vehicles are named by maximum payload. The catch here is that the jeep has a capacity to carry 500 pounds. The radio pallet weighs 400, the 2 people add about 320, extra fuel weighs 35, other field gear adds maybe 200. The Air Force version of the "quarter-ton" carries about twice its rated capacity.

The answer to this seemed to be to move the ALO and the radio pallet from his jeep into an M113 APC. This would give him the same mobility and protection as the Army forces to be near the front line.

To test this idea, we removed a radio pallet from a jeep and mounted it in the rear compartment of an M113 on the right side. This allowed us to stand in the open hatch and see the battlefield while within reach of our radios. Of course, if we had to close the hatch, we were blind. We took this prototype vehicle to Fort Bliss to test during the exercise. We called it "The FAC-in-a-Track."

In order to practice our air FAC roll during the same exercise, we rotated between flying the O-2 and riding in the M113 every other day. We had fighter support from various Air Force and National Guard units.

Going to War?

About halfway through the exercise, an emergency announcement went out on all radio systems ordering everyone to halt in place and for all officers to report to the Brigade Tactical Operations Center ASAP.

We all thought, "Oh, no. There must have been a fatal accident." There had already been one the first day. During my 2-year tour as a FAC, there were fatal accidents during almost every major exercise. We drove there quickly and gathered for a briefing from the Brigade Commander.

The commander opened with, "As of an hour ago, we are on standby to deploy." He then went on to explain that the Israelis and the Arabs have gone to war. This was what became known as the October War or Yom Kipper War in October of 1973.

Since the Fort Bliss armored division was the only unit in the US Army that was trained in desert armored fighting, we were put on alert to be sent to Israel at any moment. After explaining the situation, he told us to continue with our exercise and to take it even more seriously than normal training.

I was scheduled to drive a jeep to Biggs AAF the next morning and fly the O-2 that day. As I drove to the Biggs flight line, I was shocked to see the ramp overflowing with cargo aircraft. I remember that there were about 15 C-5's and 18 C-141's. I believe that was all the C-5's that had been delivered at that point. None were more than a few months old.

This pounded the point into our heads that there was a very serious possibility that we could move from an exercise to actual combat within a few days.

I had not seen a C-5 before that day. As I taxied past the front of one in my little O-2, I looked up and thought, "I could use that wing for a runway!"

Fortunately for us, the Israelis had no problem handling the Arabs themselves. I didn't have to fight my second war in two years. We finished our exercise in peace. The FAC-in-a-Track was so successful that it became standard in armored units. After this test, we modified the radio systems to integrate with the M-113 radio and helmet sound systems.

Met the Love of My Life

In 1974, while flying the O-2 at Bergstrom AFB, I had the luckiest day of my life since surviving the F-4 crash. I met my future wife, Barbara, when I took her for an orientation flight.

She was an Air Force ROTC cadet while a student at the University of Texas. We routinely took cadets for orientation rides to show them how the Air Force operates. In an O-2, there was no need to train them on oxygen masks or ejection seats. All they had to do was fasten the seat belt, so it was cheap and simple. We often took Army officers for orientation rides, also.

This time there were two male and two female cadets there for rides. They were sitting in folding chairs wearing flight suits and tennis shoes.

I asked who was first. They looked at each other, and no one volunteered. I thought the young lady on the end of the row looked a bit more mature and maybe older than the others. I said something memorable like, "Okay. You. Let's go."

First, we went to the Life Support shop to get her a helmet. The Tech Sergeant there told her, "Be careful riding with that guy. You might come back shorter."

She insisted that she be told why. I had to tell my ejection story. But I told her not to worry. The O-2 doesn't have an ejection seat. That didn't seem to comfort her.

When we got airborne on our 2 1/2-hour flight, I started the routine that I usually did to show the cadet how the Air Force actually used the aircraft. It's not just a joyride. Usually, the cadet gets airsick quickly,

95

and you have to fly gently. Even the bumpy Texas air from thermals often is too much for them.

With Barbara, I was able to demonstrate how we controlled fighters on ground targets. The tight maneuvering to keep the fighters and ground target both in sight can be uncomfortable for passengers. She was the only passenger that I was ever able to show 45 degree dive rocket deliveries without undue excitement. No, we did not carry live rockets with passengers. We just did the maneuver.

After that flight, she felt that she should understand more about flying, since she would be in the Air Force, so she took flying lessons and got her Private Pilot Certificate.

Shortly before her final check flight, we ran into each other at Bergstrom during the Thunderbirds' last air show in their F-4s. After we talked through the entire air show, I asked her phone number. A couple of weeks later, I called and asked her out. That didn't work out very well.

The date was for dinner on a Tuesday. My squadron normally had Tuesday through Thursday deployments each week to fighter bases for training. I wasn't scheduled for that week, but a guy who was got sick. I had to replace him, so I had to call Barbara and cancel the date. I promised to call her as soon as I returned. Years later, I found out that she told her friends about it after my call, and none of them believed me.

To her surprise, I did call and we had a prime rib dinner at Pelican's Wharf in Austin. A few days later, I went to the Austin airport and watched her final check flight. For our second date, Barbara rented a Cherokee 140, and we went flying!

I couldn't rent it, because my civilian pilot certificate was based on my AF flying in the T-37, T-38, F-4, and O-2; all multi-engine centerline thrust, so I wasn't certified for single engine.

Later, I found out that her father was in the Navy the same time as my step-father, and both were in the Pacific theater. Her father, who was also named Charles, was on the commissioning crew of the Light Cruiser CL-63, the USS Mobile, and stayed with it until it was retired to the Reserve Fleet. The Mobile was involved in several actions in the Pacific during the last two years of WW II. It was even in Tokyo Harbor for the Japanese surrender.

After the war, it carried several hundred released POWs from Nagasaki Harbor to island airfields where they could be flown home. Its last mission was to carry 1,200 Marine and Navy personnel from

Okinawa to San Diego. It was kept in the reserve fleet until being scrapped in 1959.

Ironically, both of us have Navy family backgrounds.

After several months of dating and many very long phone conversations, we decided to get married. By this time, I had received my next assignment, F-105G Wild Weasels at George AFB, CA. Barbara was scheduled to enter active duty the same time as my new assignment started.

The only problem was that the AF would not consider a joint spouse assignment unless you were actually married. We were planning to get married a few months later. The AF was going to give Barbara an assignment the other side of the country from me.

To make all this work right, we had to go to the Austin Courthouse and have a Justice of the Peace marry us. We had to delay the church wedding to the next year. Then, they agreed to send us both to George AFB. We ended up having the church wedding in the George AFB Chapel.

She wanted to work in intelligence, but the only assignment they would give her at George AFB was Avionics Maintenance Officer. This was accompanied by a "promise" that she could retrain into Intelligence in two years.

Now, we are both retired from the Air Force. I retired with 20 years active duty in 1992. She retired after almost 9 years active duty including call-up for Desert Shield/Desert Storm and a total of almost 27 years including reserve time.

Fire in the Cockpit

One week, I had to fly to Tinker AFB, OK, to support Army training at Fort Sill. I took off on a day with a 3,000'ceiling. Cloud tops were at 12,000'. I was happily cruising along completely on instruments at 8,000' halfway there when I smelled electrical smoke.

All avionics in the O-2 are mounted on a four-shelf rack at the left rear of the cabin. I looked over my shoulder and saw dense white smoke billowing out around the gyros. The two inverters beneath the gyros had small flames licking up the front of them. All the equipment for instrument flying except the radio is powered by those inverters.

Fire in the cockpit (cabin in the case of an O-2) is about the most frightening thing for a pilot. The only action I could take was to immediately slam the inverter switches to OFF. If that didn't work,

97

well, there is a fire extinguisher and I was wearing a parachute and knew how to use it.

Then, I declared an emergency with Fort Worth Center and informed them that I was descending straight ahead until clear of the clouds. Of course, that was approved. The smoke and fire stopped within a few seconds after shutting the inverters off, so I didn't need to use the fire extinguisher or the chute. Then, I opened the vent window to clear the smoke.

The descent took about five minutes. The O-2 has a floating, liquid-filled magnetic compass at the top center of the windshield as a backup for the gyro compass. A few months earlier, I was doing my annual instrument check when the check pilot asked me what I would do if I had instrument failure in instrument conditions.

I gave him a standard answer about carefully using the turn and bank needle and ball, a procedure many pilots have failed to execute.

He said, "Why not use the standby attitude indicator?" and told me about using the magnetic compass.

It's simply a plastic disk floating on some oil. Keep it level, and you're level. That wouldn't work in jets due to the large attitude movements they require, so I hadn't thought of it.

It sounded like a good idea, so I made it a point to practice a few times. This paid off as I made the descent using the mag compass as an attitude indicator. I kept the wings level by keeping the floating compass level and pulled the power back enough to establish a steady descent at a safe rate.

It was so easy that my heart rate was back to normal before I even got out of the clouds. Of course, that left me at Tinker with a broken airplane for a few days.

Lost in the Fog

On a cloudless day at Bergstrom AFB, I was scheduled for a two-hour local flight practicing visual reconnaissance. For this training, Intelligence folks give you a list of coordinates, and you are to report exactly what is at that location. All my locations were east of Bergstrom, so I headed out to enjoy the flight.

I particularly liked going to that area, because there was a private airport on a ranch where a guy refurbished B-25s. There were always a few B-25s sitting around with various parts missing. Sometimes they gave us coordinates of a specific B-25 and you had to report its condition.

About an hour into the flight, the squadron duty officer came up on our squadron frequency and announced a "weather recall." There were four of us flying around locally, so we had to return to base.

We were all baffled, because the weather was clear, but we didn't question it. Each of us thought it might be a recall to initiate an inspection or no-notice exercise. It could even be a national emergency. In any case, we headed back without more radio chatter thinking that this must be important and is being kept quiet by calling it a weather recall.

We all headed straight for Bergstrom to get on the ground ASAP. I was closest, so I arrived first. I set up for a straight-in visual approach. On final approach, the tower started announcing lowering visibility.

All I could see was clear sky, the ground below me, and a long runway ahead. What are they talking about? As I crossed the end of the runway at about 50 feet, I noticed everything was getting fuzzy. As I was touching down, I suddenly could barely see the runway right in front of me!

There was a very dense fog bank no more than 20 feet thick! Looking down through it, it wasn't noticeable. Looking horizontal after landing, you couldn't see well enough to taxi!

I carefully taxied from light to light down the right side of the runway and found the midfield turnoff. On the taxiway, I was blind. I couldn't see the grass at the edge, the blue taxiway lights, or the centerline. The Ground Controller in the tower couldn't see any of us, either. He couldn't even see our red rotating beacons.

I knew there were rows of parked O-2s in front of me, but I couldn't see anything, so I just stopped. Then, a crew chief walked up to me carrying marshalling flashlights. He walked down the taxiway centerline and led me to my parking spot.

Behind me, the next one to land tried to do the same. His crew chief couldn't find him. He followed the edge of the taxiway and stopped when he knew he was near the rows of parked aircraft.

The third to land found the taxiway and the tower sent a "Follow Me" truck out to lead him in. The truck driver quickly got lost and stopped in the grass to get out of the way.

Tower told the O-2 pilot to just shut down there and walk in. The fourth couldn't find the taxiway. He got all the way to the far end of the runway, turned onto the taxiway at the end, and parked.

We all walked in. Maintenance was able to find the other three planes and tow them in that night after the fog cleared. What a weird day.

Providential Ground Abort

The O-2 was really a militarized version of the Cessna Skymaster. All the avionics was removed and replaced with military standard equipment. A center-wing fuel tank was added to provide about an hour more flying time. Weapons stations were added with all associated switches, wiring, and gun/bombsite. Basically, it was just a slightly heavy Skymaster. It had two 210 horsepower reciprocating engines, where the Skymaster had two 235 horsepower engines. This gave the O-2 a cruise speed of only about 130 knots and a long takeoff roll for a light aircraft.

My Air Force pilot training pounded the importance of running checklists into my head to where I could not consider ever skipping an item. An incident on one of my early flights at Bergstrom proved the value of checklists.

I know of some who tended to shortcut some checks. After all, it had two engines and each had two independent magneto ignition systems. Why check all four mags each flight?

I was supposed to fly a local reconnaissance training flight at Bergstrom AFB. I prepared as usual, got my tail number assignment from the duty desk, and walked to the ramp where it was parked.

Preflight check, engine start, and taxi to the runway were routine.

The last thing before takeoff was to run the engines up one at a time while holding the brakes and do mag checks. This required turning each mag off and watching the drop in rpm on the engine. Turn the mag back on and check the other. Then do the same on the other engine. The normal drop in rpm was about 150 for each mag. The limit was 200. A drop of greater than 200 rpm required aborting the flight and returning to the ramp for maintenance.

This was the only time I saw a drop greater than 200 rpm in my 600 hours of flying the O-2. It dropped 250 on one front engine mag. This usually meant that one of the sparkplugs needed to be replaced, a ten minute job. I notified Tower that I was aborting and taxied to my parking spot on the ramp.

The Crew Chief had me shut the front engine off and leave the rear one running. He unfastened the engine cowl and pulled it off. He was going to determine which plug was bad and replace it.

Instead, his eyes opened wide and, while backing away from the aircraft, he signaled me to shut off the other engine. I did and exited the aircraft. The Crew Chief called me to come around to the left front to see what he was seeing.

Just in front of the front engine firewall is a flat bracket that holds the battery and has a metal band that goes across the battery to hold it in place. This looks just like in a car of that time period. The problem was that the metal band was just lying there on top of the battery, not screwed down. It was within an inch of shorting out the battery terminals.

About a foot underneath the battery was the fuel pump. There was a fuel leak at the fuel pump connection. Below the pump was the bottom fuselage section below the cowl. The fuel had collected in a puddle at that point. If the metal strap touched the battery terminals, it would have made sparks right over the puddle of fuel under the fuel pump and fuel lines.

That would have caused a large fire right in front of my feet with no way to extinguish it. I did have a parachute on, but this would have likely happened during takeoff roll or when lifting the nose for takeoff.

I was never more glad to abort a flight, and I *always follow the checklist*.

Practice Target Comes to Life

I sometimes deployed to Luke AFB at Phoenix, AZ, to work tactical bombing with an A-7 squadron. We used the Gila Bend Tactical Range west of Luke. It's now part of the huge Barry M. Goldwater Air Force Range. The range has several old vehicle targets mostly formed into convoys.

I was marking targets for them with WP rockets. I briefed a 4-ship flight on a convoy and rolled in to mark the lead truck. Just before I fired the rocket, the truck started moving!

I shut off my rocket switches and called off the A-7s. It appeared that the truck was people stealing scrap metal from the range, a common occurrence.

I made a couple of very low passes straight at the truck to give them the hint that they shouldn't be there. So did the A-7s. I also called the Range Control Center to report the incident. If there is a helicopter available, they usually go out and arrest the thieves. The truck eventually drove off the range.

By then, our range time was over, and the A-7's fuel was too low to get the bombing in or wait for the helicopter to guide it to the truck. Whoever was in that truck probably never knew that they were about two seconds from having a WP rocket hit on or very close to them and A-7s are extremely accurate with their 25-lb practice bombs. This also cost the Air Force thousands of dollars in lost training time.

The next year in May 1974, on a 110-degree day, a similar incident happened with another of our FACs there. AF Military Police in an SUV managed to catch one of the guys. They took him to the base, got a Spanish translator, and tried to get him to tell them how many others were there, how many vehicles they had, where were they, etc. He refused to answer any questions.

He wouldn't help the MPs find them or tell them that he was driving the only vehicle they had. A few days later, they found his five fellow scrap pickers dead from the heat with no water.

This incident is mentioned in this LA Times article: https://www.latimes.com/archives/la-xpm-1989-10-08-mn-402-story.html

Also at this range, I chased a civilian camper off the range before we could work. I think it was just lost tourists. They are allowed in most of the range, but there are warning signs near the target areas.

Engine Failure in Slow Motion

Another time that I was on this same type of practice mission, I was the one with a problem. I finished briefing a 4-ship of A-7s while circling at 10,000'. I then did my usual 45-degree dive rocket delivery and marked the lead of a convoy with a WP rocket.

I usually lose about 500-700' in that maneuver and climb right back to 10,000'. This time, when I went to full power, it climbed very slowly. I checked instruments and saw that my rear engine was only turning 2,600 RPM. Both engines should be at 2,800 RPM at full power. I tried adjusting the throttle and mixture, but it wouldn't come up to full power. If fact, it dropped to 2,500.

I told the A-7s and Range Control that I was losing power on one engine and was heading for Luke AFB. I rolled in on the truck convoy and fired all six of the rockets that were still left, then headed east.

Luke AFB is just above 1,000' elevation. The terrain between the range and Luke is as high as 3,000'. As I headed for Luke, my rear engine started losing more power. I left the range at about 9,000', but I wasn't able to maintain level flight.

The published single engine service ceiling on only front engine is 2,500'. The hot desert conditions and the fuel on board lowered that to about sea level.

When I got down to about 5,000' and was only halfway to Luke, I declared an emergency since I wasn't sure I could make it.

The comforting situation was that my route to Luke was to simply follow Interstate 10. The traffic on the highway was widely spaced. An O-2 lands at about 70 mph, so I figured I could set it down between vehicles. Bailing out of an O-2 is very difficult. You are sitting in the left seat, the only door is on the right, and there is a wing strut and rear prop to hit. If the highway wasn't clear, I would be better off landing in the desert with the gear up. There are even skids on the belly.

As I neared the base, I was down to less than 500' above I-10 and still not sure of making it. The engine was down to 1,800 RPM. Any lower and I would shut it off and feather the prop.

The runway runs north and south, so I had to head south of it and make a 90-degree left turn to land. Approaching the turn point, I was 300' above landing and still had to make a turn that I didn't have enough power to make level. I continuously tracked streets and open areas to be ready to put it down off the runway.

Tower asked me a couple of times, "Are you going to make the runway?" Both times I answered, "Don't know."

Finally, I completed the turn at about 50', right on centerline in the first 200' of the runway and made a normal landing. The tower controller keyed his mike, and I could hear applause in the tower. Maintenance told me later it was a magneto problem on that engine.

High Flying Bug

I was flying alone over central Texas returning to Bergstrom after a deployment to the west coast. I was cruising at 7,500 feet at about 125 knots. Suddenly, I glimpsed something straight ahead for less than a second before there was a very loud BANG.

On the windscreen straight in front of my face was a blob of yellow goo about four inches across with green grasshopper legs sticking out from it. I had collided head on with a huge grasshopper! I had seen grasshoppers on the ground in Texas that were as much as four inches long. However, I had no idea that they would fly that high.

Pilots in the Air Force often referred to light, propeller driven planes as "bug smashers." This was meant as a reference that they flew so low that they hit bugs like cars do. Well, some bugs aren't very low.

Of course, I got a lot of grief from the crew chief who had to clean the windscreen.

Nightmare Nellis Trip

We had two of our O-2s and three FACs deployed to Nellis AFB, NV, for a three-day exercise. While there, one of the O-2s had an electrical system failure and needed a new part. I was assigned to fly the part to Nellis using another O-2.

An O-2 carries 4 to 5 hours of fuel, but the trip west was into the wind. It was late in the day, so I had only 8 hours of a 12-hour duty day left. Getting from Bergstrom AFB, TX, to El Paso, TX, was 4 ½ hours. Another 3-hour flight would be to Luke AFB, AZ, just west of Phoenix. The last leg was a 2-hour hop from Luke to Nellis, but I had to spend the night at Luke due to mandatory crew rest.

First thing the next day, I flew to Nellis with the part. This is where the nightmare started. After a 2-hour uneventful flight, I approached Nellis in clear weather and called Nellis Approach Control. They passed the current weather information, and it differed significantly from the forecast. The wind had increased to where it would be a direct 20 knot crosswind from the right with gusts to 35 knots.

35 knots is the crosswind limit for landing and taxiing an O-2. Any higher and the twin vertical tails acted as a "weather vane" and turn the aircraft into the wind after landing

Nellis Approach allowed me to descend and approach straight in. That allowed me time to judge the wind and set up a "crab" angled into the wind to go down the runway centerline. The technique is to hold this crab until just before touchdown. Then, use rudder to align straight down the runway at touchdown.

While on final approach, I noticed that four F-4s were sitting on the taxiway at the approach end of the runway waiting for me to clear so they could take off. From my F-4 experience, I knew how critical fuel is in an F-4, so I decided I would turn off the runway at the first intersection instead of going all the way to the other end.

All of this became moot right after touchdown. I kicked the rudder to take the crab out and touched down on centerline. Right at that time, a powerful wind gust, that tower told me later was about 40 knots, hit from my right rear. I started skidding to the left as the gust raised my right wing and the right main wheel lifted a few inches off the runway. I was now below flying speed, but heading for the left side of the runway and unable to stop the skid.

My only action that could get me out of the situation was to slam the throttles full forward and take off. I got a few feet onto the grass left of the runway before I had enough speed and lifted off. Tower asked if everything was still okay. I said yes, and asked to try again.

That was approved, so I made a short pattern to the left and again arrived on short final. This time, the wind was blowing toward the runway from directly over the Nellis hangars on my right. This resulted in extreme turbulence around the end of the runway. I was being thrown around like a leaf in a whirlwind. There was no way to have enough control to safely land.

I went around again, this time asking to make a teardrop pattern and land the opposite direction on the runway. That would align me more with the wind. Tower approved immediately.

I was again bouncing around, but below about 200 feet, it was calmer. Just then, the F-4 flight lead radioed, "I think he's going to make it this time." That reminded me that they were just sitting there burning fuel, so I taxied fast and quickly cleared the runway.

It took about an hour for the maintenance crew to install the new part and fuel the aircraft I just brought. Meanwhile, I bought a sandwich and some water for the trip back to Bergstrom. The deployment commander decided to give me the repaired O-2 for the flight back to Bergstrom. We could do it in 2 4-hour flights with the tailwind, so it was planned to go from Nellis to El Paso, refuel and eat lunch, then fly to Bergstrom.

We flew as a 3-ship formation with me as number 3. The first part of the trip had a headwind instead of the expected tailwind. That slowed us down to where fuel was just enough for the leg to El Paso. To avoid the wind that would have made the trip impossible, we planned to fly at less than 1,000 feet all the way. Good plan. Seemed reasonable.

Less than an hour into the flight, I realized that I was having to use an unusually high power setting to keep up with the flight. I checked everything and discovered that the flap handle was about half way down. Sure enough, the flaps were half way down causing a lot of drag. I was puzzled how that happened, but I raised the flaps and everything was normal.

However, the handle wouldn't stay up. It wasn't practical to hold it, and that would have probably burned out the drive motor, so I had to let it go down and push it back up every minute or two. This used more fuel than planned.

About an hour later, I again started slowing down. This time, it was the rear cowl flaps. These are doors on the sides of the engine cowling. They are electric like the flaps. The cowl flaps are opened while on the ground to allow more cooling air to the engine. The switch was in the closed position and nothing would close them. That added a lot more drag and required a lot more power to stay with the flight. If I used enough power for normal speed, I wouldn't have enough fuel to reach El Paso.

The other two planes continued on to El Paso while I dropped behind and we kept in contact via radio. I was seriously worried that I wasn't going to make it. I selected alternate landing spots along the way and flew over each of them. Finally, I landed at El Paso about 20 minutes after the others and with only a few minutes of fuel left.

The cowl flap problem was fixed by the maintenance crew within minutes. The flap switch was a bigger problem and would have to wait for Bergstrom maintenance. While they were working on the cowl flaps, I walked around to check over the rest of the O-2. I was shocked to find that both main tires had red tread showing over significant areas. During the deployment at Nellis, they had been flying with strong crosswinds and wore the tires down to where my landing at El Paso went into the red. Tires have to be changed at that point to avoid a blowout on the next landing.

While the aircraft were being fueled, I pointed out the tires to the deployment leader and told him they had to be changed before the next flight. He asked me if I was afraid to fly it. I said not really, but it would be a violation of safety rules to fly it. He tried to get one of the other FACs to fly it, but they all refused and backed me. He also decided not to fly it himself.

I rode back to Bergstrom in the one empty seat in a good aircraft. The next day, another Bergstrom FAC flew another O-2 to El Paso with two tires and a maintenance sergeant who could fix the flap switch. El Paso had a maintenance team that could change the tires.

Winter Alaska Exercise

Three of our Tactical Air Control Party (TACP) teams were deployed to Alaska for a 9-day exercise starting at the end of January 1974. This was on the ground with an air mobile battalion. Air mobile means an infantry unit that moves around via helicopter. Ten UH-1

106

"Huey" choppers were assigned to my battalion. My "operations center" was a normally a jeep with four radios.

During operations with the air mobile unit, I operated from the back seat of a Huey using one of the Huey FM radios to talk to the Army and a portable UHF radio to talk to aircraft.

We initially deployed to Fort Richardson, just northeast of Anchorage, AK; an all-day flight from Bergstrom AFB in the back of a C-130. We arrived at Anchorage just in time to watch the start of the Iditarod Dog Sled Race. There was no snow in Anchorage, so they trucked in enough to create a snow path from the starting line to a point outside of downtown. There they trucked the teams several miles to where the snow trail started. Melting was not a problem with temperatures around zero.

Whiteout C-130 Landing

Later, I rode in the back of a C-130 from Fort Richardson to Fort Greely. The Fort Greely runway was covered with snow. I couldn't see much from the back, just a little out of the windshield looking through the cockpit.

After getting out of the airplane, I asked the pilot how they land. All I could see was a whiteout. He said it's a normal landing until touchdown. Brakes won't stop you, so you use reverse thrust, constantly adjusting thrust on each side to hold the runway heading.

The reverse thrust causes the whiteout. You use the throttles to hold the heading until stopping. Then, pull the props to neutral and wait for the snow to settle. At that point, you can see where you are, so you taxi onto the runway or taxiway, whichever is more convenient.

The next day, I rode a Huey back to Fort Richardson where we met up with our Army unit and convoyed north to Fort Greely, about 100 miles southeast of Fairbanks. The only distraction was that our convoy was delayed about 15 minutes while a herd of Bison crossed the highway.

The exercise was in the mountains southeast of Fort Greely. We set up our hex tents near the Battalion command tent. No heaters were allowed, due to fire hazard. I don't think the temperature inside the tent ever got above zero. The weather forecast for that 22-hour night was for -45F.

We figured we would be okay with three people in an insulated hex tent in mountain sleeping bags stuffed inside arctic sleeping bags. They call them "Arctic shells." I slept in my long underwear plus the extreme cold underwear that we called waffle weave. I also tucked my uniform in the bag around me so that it would provide more insulation and be warm in the morning.

Cold Surprise

Around 0500, I woke up. I needed some bladder relief, so I decided to take a quick run outside the tent. I put on my arctic boots and unzipped the tent. I took two quick steps outside the tent in my long underwear before the arctic cold smacked me.

I stopped instantly, dived back inside, and zipped the tent. Then, I zipped myself back inside my still-warm sleeping bag and shivered for half an hour.

It turned out that the forecast was for the air base and did not take into consideration the higher elevation of the exercise area. The actual temperature was -65 with a chill factor to -85. That was 60 degrees colder than I had ever experienced before! Ears freeze in less than 30 seconds.

Operating in those conditions is nearly impossible. I had six F-4s supporting me with CAS. Unfortunately, they were deployed to Elmendorf AFB, near Anchorage, AK, from Homestead AFB, FL.

There was no hangar space available, so all the planes were parked on the open ramp. The planes were not properly prepared for the cold, and the maintenance crews had never worked wearing anything heavier than a T-shirt.

Parkas and Arctic gloves made their work frustrating and very slow. Half the sorties scheduled never got airborne. Of those that took off, half aborted with hydraulic failures. If one aircraft in a 2-ship has a hydraulic failure emergency, the other one has to escort it back to base. Almost none of them were able to work a target.

I also had two RF-4s for taking photos. Their maintenance chief had been stationed in Alaska with an F-4 unit years earlier. Before deploying, he had his men replace all hydraulic seals with new, more flexible ones. He also had all lubrication changed to a lighter weight oil. They flew every sortie as scheduled.

Chopper Down

Our main infantry attack required my unit to do an assault landing in a large clearing with all ten Huey's simultaneously. There was over two feet of snow, so everyone went into whiteout conditions the last 50 feet before landing.

I was in the center of the group. The Huey on the right drifted right during the whiteout and hit trees with the rotor. That spun them into the ground and slammed the transmission into the back wall of the cabin, bulging the wall forward a foot.

There were five troops sitting on the rear bench seat wearing seat belts that were bolted to the floor, not the seat. All five received significant back injuries, with the one in the center severe.

The battalion commander's Huey had its arctic heater fail, so he commandeered my Huey. He gave me his to use as a makeshift ambulance to get the injured soldiers to the hospital at Fairchild AFB. It took three trips in the unheated Huey while guys with back injuries were held motionless flat on the floor by those of us who were okay.

ALO Down

A major part of the attack was by our airborne element. They jumped from C-130s on a -35 degree day. The Brigade ALO, a Major, had his helmet strap break when he jumped due to being soaked with sweat, then frozen.

The airflow caused his helmet to trail several inches above his head. When his chute opened, the helmet slammed into the bridge of his nose, making a large gash from eye to eye. It bled a lot, and the blood covered his face and froze before he got to the ground. Blood froze his eyes shut.

He called for help, and the first guy to get to him turned away and vomited. He was air evacuated by a Huey. I had to cover his Brigade ALO position for that attack. After being cleaned up and bandaged, he was able to get back to work and didn't look so scary. I was happy not to be jump qualified.

REFORGER 1973

During my time as a Battalion ALO, I participated in a REFORGER exercise. That stands for Redeployment of Forces To Germany. REFORGER was an annual exercise implemented to be ready in case the peace in Europe didn't hold.

Each year, a few Army units would deploy for a month and return to the US. Most of the vehicles and equipment were stored in warehouses in Germany. The deployment included drawing all wartime equipment out of storage, two-weeks of field maneuvering, cleaning and repairing everything, and returning it all to storage.

The Air Force chose not to pay for a duplicate set of TACP equipment, so we had to airlift our vehicles along with our personnel. I was scheduled on a C-141.

It first flew to Bergstrom AFB to pick us up. Then, it flew to the Salina, KS, airport near Fort Riley to pick up the TACP personnel and vehicles that were stationed at Fort Riley.

From there, it flew nonstop to Rheine-Main AB in Germany. When we offloaded everything, my clothes bag with all my clothes and my A-3 bag with all my field gear were missing! They were nowhere to be found, so I had to borrow unmarked uniforms and field gear from the TACP detachment there. I also had to buy a shaver, civilian clothes, coat, and shoes to wear when not on duty.

REFORGER was always scheduled during October. During our two weeks in the field, it rained every day. Not just a little, but steady moderate rain day and night. The mud was so deep that our M-60 tanks were getting stuck in mud to the top of their tracks.

Our jeeps wouldn't always make it through the mud to keep up with the Army. I had to have an Army vehicle pull me out several times. We quit trying to set up our tents in the mud and just slept in our jeeps. We expanded the jeep roof with ponchos to keep dry.

Remember, I was there to plan, coordinate, and control CAS with the Army. The worst part of the weather was that it was too bad to fly. We finally had a day that was good enough to fly over the exercise area for a few hours, but the air bases over 100 miles away were well below minimum ceiling and visibility, so we *still* couldn't get any CAS.

The Army decided we were useless. Several years later, the more maneuverable A-10 was able to work in those conditions.

Upon return home to Bergstrom AFB, I started making phone calls to find my missing bags. I found out that the C-141 was from Dover AFB, DE. A Dover crew flew it to Bergstrom to pick us up and on to Salina, KS. Due to crew rest requirements, The crew was changed at Salina to a crew from Norton AFB, CA, to make the same-day trip to Germany.

I managed to contact the navigator from Norton at his home in Lake Arrowhead, CA. He told me that the Dover crew had spent the night at Salina in the Holiday Inn. All of their luggage had been removed from a pallet in the aircraft and taken to the motel. Each guy picked up his own bags from the pile in the motel lobby.

I called the Holiday Inn and asked if they had unclaimed bags that fit the description I gave them. When the answer was yes, I told him to unzip them and see what is just inside under the zipper.

He opened them and said there was a copy of my orders for the trip. Putting them there was standard procedure to identify field gear. No one had bothered to look inside. They just put the bags into their baggage storage room. I had to send a check to the Holiday Inn to pay for shipping the bags to me. A few years later, they started providing heavy paper tags with string to tie onto the bags.

This entire deployment was a disappointment due to the weather, and not having my clothes and equipment. At the end, I fit a 4-day bus trip around Bavaria and Switzerland in before the flight home. This was worth the trip.

Uncommanded Rocket Firings

The O-2 has two hardpoints under each wing for carrying weapons. Each hardpoint can carry a Minigun pod or a rocket pod. The rocket pod holds seven 2.75 inch rockets. In combat for target marking, the rockets are loaded with White Phosphorus (WP) warheads. For training, the rockets are loaded with an inert metal warhead.

During a deployment to George AFB, one of our squadron pilots was scheduled to go to Cuddeback Range with a load of seven inert rockets to practice on a controlled range with scored targets. Using triangulation from two manned towers, the Range crew would score each rocket shot or practice bomb drop, and the Range Control Officer would give the pilot the direction and distance of impact from target center. A direct hit in the center is called a "shack."

As he approached the range, he radioed Range Control to let them know he was inbound so they could man the towers and be ready. Then, he turned on the switch for the left wing station that had the rocket pod, and turned on the Master Arm switch. He lined up on the line leading to the target so that the Range Control Tower would be on the left as he reached the target.

The procedure for range entry was to fly this path, report in to Range Control, pass over the target, and begin a left rectangular pattern firing a rocket in a 45 degree dive at the target on each pass. Range Control would announced the score after each pass. Everything was fine until he tried to report in to Range Control.

Rockets are fired by using your left forefinger to press a red button inside a half-inch ring on the left handle of the left control yoke. To the right of that ring is the microphone switch for the radio. It is simply a metal pin about 1/16 inch diameter that sticks up half an inch. You push it forward with your left thumb to transmit.

He pushed the radio switch to let Control know he was approaching.

To his complete shock, *a rocket fired*!

Since he was still flying level, the rocket headed well past the target and about 100 feet right of the Range Control Tower. While it was still in flight, he pressed the mic switch again to warn them. *Whooosh! Another rocket fired.*

This time, he realized that the mic switch must be shorting into the firing button. He turned off the Master Arm switch and wing station switch. Then, he flew straight toward the target again and pressed the mic switch. No rocket. Good.

He told Range Control what happened and got permission to fire the rest of his rockets to be safe going back to base.

We had to stand down all O-2s a few days until a fix was installed on all of them.

Hangar Fire Disaster

While in the 702nd TASS, my primary additional duty was Mobility Officer. Since the squadron had a sole mission of being ready to deploy on short notice with any Army battalion west of the Mississippi River, mobility was a huge responsibility.

We had 106 jeeps with trailers. Each jeep had the TACP 4-radio pallet. The trailer carried a generator, fuel, and field gear. The jeeps had half a tank of fuel, ready to be driven onto cargo aircraft with the trailers attached.

The O-2s can't fly far enough to get themselves out of the US, so they had to be dismantled, put in wooden boxes, and shipped on cargo aircraft. For each O-2, we had two wing boxes and a tail box. The fuselage had a partial box.

At the end of the flight line O-2 ramp, there was a huge wooden hangar built during the early months of WWII. It was the oldest building on base. The hangar was the responsibility of the base, but our squadron owned everything in it.

We kept 96 jeeps with trailers in the hangar ready to deploy. Several others used daily for training were also there. The hangar also contained all the O-2 boxes, all the maintenance shops, all the aircraft and vehicle maintenance records, the battery shop, the tire shop, and extra personal equipment.

Thanksgiving weekend of 1974, I woke up about dawn and turned on the television. The local station had just broken into programming with a special report. The live video was clearly *my hangar on fire*!

Nobody had called me yet (no cell phones in 1974). I grabbed a uniform, jumped in my car, and drove the 20 minutes to the base. I could see the smoke all the way there.

A heater in one corner of the hanger, which was the only heater running, had caught fire. It quickly spread to the wooden wall and ceiling. An MP guard walking around the area saw the first smoke and immediately radioed the fire station, which was only a block away. They were on scene within five minutes.

By then, most of the building was burning with fuel tanks on the jeeps exploding, 55-gallon drums of cleaning solvent exploding, and piles of tires burning, in addition to the old wood hangar walls and roof.

An MP with a truck hooked a chain to the large locked door and pulled it off to get access. By then, some of the squadron enlisted men had arrived. They managed to pull five jeeps out before it was impossible to go back in.

When I arrived, the hangar was a 3-foot layer of flaming rubble. You could see lumps of melted metal in neat rows where each jeep was parked. The fire burned for more than a day. All was lost except those five jeeps.

The jeeps and radio pallets were no longer being built. There was a new version about to begin deployment with manufacture just beginning.

The Air Force had just started a 2-year program to replace each O-2 with an OV-10. There was one other O-2 unit. It was at Shaw AFB. We brought some of their tools and parts to Bergstrom to keep the planes flying. We also borrowed a few of their jeeps for training.

91 of our TACP vehicles were destroyed. The 5 pulled out of the hangar and 6 that were in a maintenance shop survived. The big truth was that the Air Force did not have a TACP to deploy with half the Army for over a year! Luckily, they weren't needed.

Thud target fixation

I deployed to George AFB, CA, to work with the F-105 Thunderchief (known as the "Thud") squadrons there practicing CAS on a tactical range. I had no idea that those Thuds would be my next assignment.

I marked targets with WP rockets and briefed the pilots on the target, which was an aircraft in a revetment. After dropping BDU-33 25 pound practice bombs, they were to do 30-degree strafe with their 20mm cannons.

Number three rolled in for his strafe pass and lined up on the briefed target. His flight path looked good, so I called, "Cleared Hot." However, he kept diving at the target past the point where he should have been shooting. I called, "Go dry and pull up." (If you shoot too late, you can hit ricocheting rounds.)

He continued toward the target. As he got way too low, I started yelling, "PULL UP! PULL UP! PULL UP!" The flight leader also started calling to pull up. At the very last second, the pilot realized his situation and pulled up very hard. He passed less than 20 feet over the target, leaving a rooster tail in the dust from his jet blast. I told him to stay high and dry for the rest of the passes.

Back at the base, he thanked me over and over and said he had no idea why it happened. We think it was a common situation called "target fixation." The George Thuds are all Wild Weasels. They mostly practice with their anti-radiation missiles and rarely strafe. Clearly, this training was needed.

I never found out if the EWO in the back seat had also called for a pull up. He should have been giving verbal altitude calls and should have called the attack off after passing the expected shooting altitude. The EWO really has little to do during strafing and rarely practices it. This showed the importance of the WSO monitoring an attack.

Landing an O-2 with No Flight Controls

This was not me, but it was an amazing feat in an O-2 shortly after I left the squadron.

When I started flying the O-2, we were required to wear a back-pack parachute at all times. There wasn't even a seatback cushion in the seats, so the chute functioned as a cushion. During my time there, the rule was changed. They added a removable seatback cushion and did not require wearing the chute for point to point flights. It was only required when actually controlling fighters, during test flights, or in combat.

Two of the 702nd FACS were returning together to Bergstrom AFB from a deployment in an O-2. They didn't have parachutes. I'm not sure how far out they were, but before arriving at Bergstrom, they suffered a catastrophic failure of the attachment of the control yoke mechanism to the main control tube. This made both control yokes useless. There was now no way to move the ailerons or elevator, leaving no roll or pitch control.

The electric trim system worked, but has very little control authority and moves slowly. It was enough to maintain level flight, but not to land.

The two pilots started discussing what to do and declared an emergency to get traffic priority. They then contacted the 702nd squadron duty desk to discuss the situation with the most experienced pilots available.

They started to try different control methods while still at several thousand feet altitude. All pilots know that an aircraft trimmed for level flight will climb or descend by adding or reducing power with the engine throttle. This was a way to descend at a controlled rate, but is not as responsive as the elevator.

The rudder was not affected, so the rudder pedals worked normally. Therfore, the rudder could be used to make gentle turns. Without ailerons, this would be uncoordinated turns that would have to be done gradually.

They decided that it would be easier to maintain control if one of them controlled descent and climb using the throttles, and the other used the rudder pedals to steer. They lowered the landing gear and flaps and slowed to near a normal final approach speed, about 75 knots, while adjusting the power to maintain level flight.

Then, they practiced reducing power just enough to descend and used the rudder to maintain a straight line. After practicing several times, they were able to fly at final approach speed and simulate a landing at a safe altitude.

Bergstrom tower cleared the airspace so that they could start several miles away and stabilize on final approach well short of the runway. The runway offered 10,000 feet of landing space, and the O-2 would only need a few hundred feet of it, so they aimed for the middle.

For a normal landing, the pilot would pull the power to idle shortly before touchdown and use the elevator to raise the nose for a smooth

115

touchdown at about 60 knots. In this case, they couldn't raise the nose, so they had to use a small increase in power just before touchdown to slow the descent rate.

Their two-man control technique worked well, resulting in a smooth landing.

After touchdown the throttles were pulled to idle and rudders steered just like a normal landing.

I'm not sure, but I heard that they received Air Medals for this heroic landing

Departure Crashes #6 & 7

A couple of months after leaving Bergstrom, one of the Bergstrom O-2s was at the Nellis AFB Range Complex in Nevada and crashed into the end of a blind canyon. When it was discovered missing, a search was launched.

During that search, another O-2 flew into the same canyon and crashed into the end. The single pilot in the first aircraft and the two in the second were all killed. Of course, I knew all of them and considered them good pilots.

It was discovered that the canyon, when entered at low altitude, appeared to have a level floor. However, it was not obvious that the sky seen above the far end was not the horizon, but actually well above the horizon, because the canyon floor gradually rose in that direction. The floor rose faster than an O-2 could climb and the canyon was too narrow to turn around. By the time a pilot realized the optical illusion, it was too late to avoid the ground. An F-100 pilot fell for the same illusion several years earlier. It was decided that the problem needs to be in the education of all pilots. These accidents resulted in a major training briefing on optical illusions that had to be given to all AF pilots.

Two A-7s Down

I'm not going to count this as a departure crash, but I want to mention another set of accidents. We had a Captain O-2 FAC who was a terrible pilot. I don't know how, but before I was there, he was selected to be an Instructor Pilot in the O-2 squadron.

I once deployed with him to Fort Sill, OK. He flew left seat, not acting as an IP, while I was in the right seat. I hated that, because flying in the right seat didn't count as flight time unless you were an IP.

116

He flew all the way. He didn't keep his altitude very accurately, and I pointed out heading errors a couple of times. When landing, he flared way too early, nearly stalled 20 feet above the runway, put the nose down to recover, and got into a pilot-induced-oscillation that was about to slam us into the pavement.

I grabbed the controls, yelled "I have the aircraft!", added power, stabilized the descent, and made a smooth landing. Getting on the ground several hundred feet long was not a big deal on the long runway. There is no doubt in my mind that I avoided an accident that day. That was the only time I ever flew an O-2 from the right seat.

I privately reported the incident to our squadron commander but did not make a written report. I found out they were already watching him, but no action was taken.

Everyone who goes to a 2-year FAC assignment is guaranteed a fighter assignment next. Not long after the incident with me, he received an assignment to an A-7 unit. First, he had to attend A-7 training. The A-7 does not have a 2-seat version for training, so all flights are solo.

Midway through his training, he lost control while making a routine join-up with the flight. He didn't handle the situation properly and got into a spin. He couldn't recover and ejected.

A Flight Evaluation Board (FEB) was held to decide if he should keep his wings. The board decided to give him another chance and sent him back to finish the training.

During the FEB, the colonel chairing the board asked, "Why didn't you deploy the drag chute?" At that time, nearly all Air Force jet fighters and bombers had drag chutes for stopping after their normal fast landings. These can also help recover from a spin. The Air Force had only recently bought the A-7. The Navy designed it for operation from aircraft carriers. A hook performs the function of the drag chute for the Navy. After hearing that the answer was that the A-7 doesn't have a drag chute, the colonel might have been too embarrassed to take someone's wings.

The rest of this story is at Shaw AFB, SC. This guy went to his operational squadron at Shaw. A few months later, he was making a level low altitude delivery of a practice bomb at their bombing range. The range is on the coast, with a barge in the water as the target.

After dropping the bomb, he continued level at about 200 feet, but rolled left a bit into a gentle turn when he should have still been level and going straight ahead. This is typical of someone trying to look back over his shoulder to see the bomb impact instead of waiting for the score from the range controller.

During that turn, he descended too much and hit the water at 500 knots. This was a death and two destroyed aircraft that should have been avoided. There were several points in this guy's career that demonstrated he should have been grounded. I'm just glad that he was in a single-seat aircraft.

Holloman AFB, New Mexico

https://www.holloman.af.mil/

July 1975

Jet Recurrency Training

My next assignment was to the F-105. Since I had been flying the O-2 at 125 knots for 2 years, I had to attend Jet Recurrency Training at Holloman AFB for 2 weeks.

Barbara and I had just been married, so we drove there together. She refused to count it as a honeymoon. The drives from Austin, TX, to Holloman AFB, NM, and back were great sightseeing. Neither of us had been there before.

It was a long trip on isolated 2-lane highways. Going through a wooded area on the way west, a Golden Eagle swooped down coming the opposite direction. It leveled at windshield height and came straight at our faces. At the very last second as we ducked, it climbed just enough to miss the roof. The last two hours were in desert.

We rented an old, one-bedroom house trailer for the two weeks. Barbara turned on the "swamp cooler" air cooler in the ceiling. Apparently, the trailer was empty for some time, so the cooler was full of desert dust. Barbara got it straight in the face when the cooler turned on. After the desert drive to get there, she wanted nothing other than to get away ASAP.

Jet recurrency was in the T-38. About the time I arrived, the Air Force learned an expensive lesson about accommodating women in the force. Hair was not allowed below the top of a shirt collar according to AF Reg 35-10. Long hair was dangerous around much of the equipment on a flight line and in the maintenance hangars. The new reg allowed women to have longer hair, but it must be worn up above the collar when in uniform. There was a provision that allowed

118

wearing the long hair under a short wig while in uniform. Hats were not allowed on the flight line due to the possibility of sucking one into an engine.

The first T-38 female crew chief was at Holloman. One day, she was marshalling a T-38 that was about to taxi to the runway. The student pilot gave the "chocks out" signal (thumbs in front of his face pointed in opposite directions and moving them apart), and she bent over to pull the chocks from the nose gear.

The student pilot didn't wait long enough for her to clear before starting to push the power up. The aircraft did not move, but the increased suction pulled her wig off and into the left engine. That did half a million dollars of damage and required another revision to the reg banning wigs from the flight line the same as hats.

The idea of jet recurrency was to get your mind and feel of the aircraft back up to jet speeds and review jet instrument procedures. I loved getting to fly the T-38 again! Unfortunately, I was so happy back in it that I finished the ten-sortie course in six. I cheated myself out of four flights. At least, I got Barbara out of the desert four days early.

On the way back to Bergstrom, an owl landed on the road just in front of us. I knocked it's head off with the front bumper. Bummer!

Since Barbara was just entering active duty, she had to go to her parents' home in Nanty Glo, PA, for some leave and to pick up her personal things and to buy a car. After this, she headed to Lowry AFB, Denver CO, for Avionics Maintenance Officer training while I was at McConnell AFB, Kansas, for F-105 training.

McConnell Air Force Base, Kansas
https://en.wikipedia.org/wiki/McConnell_Air_Force_Base
April 1975

This is an F-105D that I flew.

Arrival Crash #7

A few days before I arrived, an F-105D (single seat version) lost all oil pressure 20 minutes away from the base. The F-105 engine is known to last about 18 minutes without oil. The pilot headed straight for McConnell, since it was the closest place to land. He was about half a mile from touchdown when the engine seized.

That's not only loss of thrust, but also all hydraulics and most electrics. His only choice was to eject immediately. The aircraft landed just short of the 1,000-foot overrun, sheared the landing gear off, and slid all the way to the runway on its belly.

Unfortunately, a lady driving a car with her baby daughter in a child seat in the back ignored the red stoplight on the road that crosses the overrun. The F-105 scooped the front of her car up into the left engine air intake. The fire department had already arrived due to the oil loss emergency, so they were on scene immediately. They got the people out of the car, and no fire started. The lady was very seriously injured, but the baby was unharmed.

Thud Training

My new assignment was to fly the F-105G Wild Weasel aircraft at George AFB, CA, where the last three F-105G squadrons were. However, the only F-105 Thunderchief (known as the "Thud") training squadron was an Air National Guard squadron at McConnell AFB, KS. I had to go there for three months where I would train in the F-105D and F.

The F-105 was a very sleek design with a very pointed fuselage and thin wings. From the forward aspect, it's even hard to see at a distance. This turned out to be a problem and a blessing. It made it difficult for enemy aircraft radars to see it from the front. That's a major advantage.

At that time, the only precision approach for landing in very bad weather was the Ground Controlled Approach (GCA). A radar van was placed beside the center of the runway. The GCA controller sat in that van and watched the aircraft on his radar. The controller talked the pilot down all the way by telling him his position from the correct flight path: "above glide path," "turn left to heading182," etc. Of course, this is only needed in bad weather.

It turned out that the F-105 was so stealthy that the GCA controller could not see it in the rain, right when needed the most. The solution to this was to mount an aluminum corner reflector box on the nose gear strut right above the tire. The box is angled so that when the aircraft is nose high at low speed, it points right at the GCA radar. It's attached to the strut, so it's retracted with the nose gear. For looks and drag reduction, it has a rounded fiberglass cover. The cover is normally painted the color code of the maintenance flight that is responsible for that aircraft. Also, the last three digits of the tail number are normally painted on it.

The F-105F and G have a rear cockpit, but you can't see forward from it, so most training is done in the single-seat D with the instructor chasing in another D. Since the F-105D is single seat, pilots are required to memorize all checklists. We had to do five hours of "cockpit time" getting familiar with it and running through checklists. While doing that, I counted 250 controls. That's switches, knobs, buttons, and levers, but not including dozens of circuit breakers.

After several days of academics, pilots get two back seat flights in an F to get the feel of the aircraft in simple maneuvers. It includes simulating a traffic pattern and final approach on instruments, but at 5,000 feet.

They never built an F-105 simulator. This meant that you had to learn to fly a very fast aircraft that is one of the most difficult to land in the Air Force in an actual aircraft! That cockpit time procedure training was now real, and your life depended upon doing it right.

Then, it's first takeoff and landing *solo* in a D model. Takeoff takes nearly a mile of runway to reach the 192 knot rotation speed and more to reach liftoff speed. The Thud is a great aircraft at high speed, but it does not want to fly much below 300 knots.

The operational version of the aircraft progressed through models B, D, F, and G. Each new model added weight. The F added six feet to the length for a second cockpit plus an extended rear section to balance the center of gravity.

The catch was that the engine and wings were the same in all models. This resulted in the F and G being underpowered and with a very high wing loading.

Final approach speed for the B was 186 knots, the D was 191 knots, the F was 196 knots, and the G was 201 knots. In addition, you had to add one knot for every thousand pounds of fuel and external stores. That would add at least 5 and maybe 30 to final speed. A perfect landing would touchdown about 30 knots below final approach speed after a half-mile long flare, or roundout, as the Navy would say. Perfect was rare.

In contrast, the F-4 and F-111 final approach is around 130 knots. After all, they were designed for an aircraft carrier.

It takes a lot of finesse to make a good landing in a Thud. Then, you stop it by keeping the nose up for aero braking, using the drag chute, and being very careful with brakes that overheat easily.

Barbara visited me at McConnell AFB for a few days on her way to Lowry AFB, CO, for Avionics Maintenance Officer training. She happened to be there to watch my first flight in the D.

She had her pilot license by then, and fully understood what she was watching. Since the Thud touches down at over 170 knots, you can't do touch and go landings due to rapid heating of the tires and brake assembly. The first flight was practicing landing patterns at altitude, then several low approaches to the runway, then one full stop. The sole objective of the flight was to successfully takeoff and land.

I did 12 low approaches. Afterward, Barbara told me what she saw on each one and what I did wrong, too high, too low, too fast, just right. She was exactly right on all of them.

That first full stop landing in a Thud is about as much excitement as you can get flying, unless, of course, you have to land on an aircraft carrier. ☺

One of the final things you do in F-105 training is a no-flap landing in case one day they won't go down. That's a 240 knot final approach! Have fun stopping! It's only practiced once, since it is hard on tires and brakes.

Thud Refueling

A highlight of the training was air-to-air-refueling. Of course, I had done hundreds of them in the F-4, all with a KC-135 tanker. The main difference was that the F-4 refueling port is on the top of the fuselage about seven feet behind the pilot's head very near the aircraft center of gravity. The aircraft flies very stable in that position while connected to the tanker.

The refueling port in the Thud is about six feet straight in front of the pilot's face and slightly left of center. It's so close to the nose that it tends to push the nose of the Thud sideways. This makes it very difficult to hold position.

Also, when you disconnect, it always spills a little fuel straight into the Thud engine intakes. The fuel goes right through the engine okay, but some is captured by the bleed air system and dumped into the cockpit pressurization and air conditioning system, filling the cockpit with fumes. To avoid that, we had to shut off the pressurization and heat before refueling. That's uncomfortable for the ears and cold at our usual 24,000' refueling altitude.

The Thud is unique in that it can refuel both using the Air Force boom system and the Navy probe and drogue system. With the boom system, the pilot just flies the proper formation position on the tanker, and the boom operator moves the boom into position and inserts it into the port.

With the Navy system, which most other countries use, too, the tanker reels out a hose with a "basket" on the end. This is the drogue. The receiver pilot extends a probe and manually fly's his aircraft to put the probe into the drogue. On the Thud, the probe is about the 10 o'clock position on the left side of the nose.

What made this truly exciting was that the only tanker available on the day we had to do probe and drogue refueling was an old Air National Guard KC-97.

The problem was that the KC-97 couldn't fly fast enough for a Thud. With all engines at full power, the KC-97 could only get to 240 knots. We normally refueled at 310 knots. 240 is final approach speed for a Thud with the flaps up. You have to lower one half or one third flaps in order to have enough maneuverability at that speed. Since we still had most of our fuel when doing this, the Thuds were barely able to stay level, and the controls were very sloppy.

At one point, we flew through the top of a cumulus cloud where there was some turbulence. Our Thuds couldn't handle that at such a slow speed, and we all stalled. We all pushed the nose down and added a little power to regain control. Okay, we're flying again, but now the tanker was behind us. It took several minutes of large "S" turns to get back into refueling position.

Our entire 4-ship had great difficulty making good contacts, but we all managed to finally transfer some fuel to qualify.

Departure Crash #8

A few weeks after I left, a wing broke off one of the F-105D's, killing a guy who had been in my pilot training class in 1971. More on that later.

George Air Force Base, California, Again

https://en.wikipedia.org/wiki/George_Air_Force_Base

June 1975

F-105G that I flew is now in the AF Museum in Ohio.

Getting a Wild Weasel assignment required 500 hours of fighter time, combat experience, flight lead qualified, and recommendations from three senior officers. I was a little short on the fighter time, but they waived it due to my recommendation letters. When I was in Vietnam,

124

the Thuds were flying the Wild Weasel mission leading our Linebacker missions.

Unfortunately, when I got there, I discovered I was the youngest pilot in the Weasel squadrons, and most of the others had flown the Weasels in Vietnam. I had no chance for important additional duties. Also, I wouldn't lead many flights.

Moving to George AFB

Barbara found a VW Beetle that was a few years old, but only had 5,000 miles on it. It was a classic case of a little old lady owning a car that was only used once a week for her son to drive her to church.

Barbara had to drive from PA to Lowry AFB, CO, at Denver to attend training for Avionics Maintenance Officer. By the time she finished that, I had moved to George AFB and rented a tiny apartment until we could get a house.

When Barbara drove to George, she was surprised that it was a two-day drive through bare rock mountains and desert to get there. She described the area as "God ran out of ideas."

Then she said that she would have thought harder about this whole thing if she knew she would end up in the middle of the desert. I assured her that it was only one more hour of driving to be in Los Angeles. She found that hard to believe until we actually made our first of many trips through Cajon Pass over the San Bernardino mountains and into the coastal cities.

Arrival Crash #8

The wing breaking off crash was repeated two months later at another base, although I didn't know the pilot. In both accidents, the wing broke off bending up, and the fuselage broke in half at that point, causing the other wing to also break off. All four parts instantly folded up and smashed together with the vertical tail hitting directly into the cockpit. The pilots never had a chance.

The result was the grounding of all F-105s while the problem was fixed. There was a hidden crack forming at the point where the wing attached to the fuselage. The worst crack was in the main fuselage bulkhead where the wing attaches.

While inspecting for these cracks, they discovered cracks in some wings. Nearly all the Thuds had the crack. Any of them could have broken any time they pulled a few G's. The rest of us were just lucky.

Most of the Thuds were repaired, but on several, the crack was too deep, so they were permanently grounded. In fact, there were a few cases where wings were swapped between active aircraft and aircraft on permanent static display to get a good wing on a flyable aircraft.

We had 36 F-105G aircraft when I arrived. The G was an F with the electronics for finding radars and attacking air defenses added. The guy in the back was an Electronics Warfare Officer (EWO) instead of WSO.

Over 40 had been lost in Vietnam, and all of those left had patches all over from years of combat. There were three Wild Weasel squadrons sharing what was really two squadrons of aircraft.

We were down to 24 aircraft, 18 flyable, by the time I left four years later. The aircraft were very unreliable due to wear and tear and lack of spare parts. Everyone loved flying it due to its challenging mission, the challenge of flying it well, the exhilarating low altitude speed of over 700 knots, and the prestige of being selected for the assignment. We could routinely use 640 knots for attacks where the F-4 would be at 500.

First Daughter

Of course, the best part of this assignment was the birth of Gwen, our first daughter. She was born at the base hospital after Barbara had several false alarms over a couple of weeks. Barbara was an Avionics Maintenance Officer commanding a unit of several hundred avionics technicians. She was only given one week off after the C-section birth! Tough lady.

Chief Parroff

When Barbara started as the Chief of the Avionics Maintenance Branch at George, she worked with Chief Master Sergeant Paul Parroff. He looked like the TV character Captain Kangaroo except with a cigar. He was a great guy and friendly with everyone.

I visited Barbara's office, and she introduced me to him. We discovered that he was stationed at Kunsan AB, Korea, the same time as me.

Barbara asked him if he was there when an F-4 crashed on takeoff in March, 1973. He said "Oh, My God! I actually saw it happen!" Then he described the entire sequence of the accident very accurately.

When he finished, Barbara pointed out that I was the pilot. He was amazed. He shook my hand and said he was honored to meet me.

Then, he told us that immediately after the crash, he had all the maintenance crews do a full toolbox check to make sure all tools were accounted for. Accidents are sometimes caused by lost tools, such as the T-37 at Laredo just before my pilot training.

Chief Parroff died of lung cancer just before we left George.

Flight Test School Students

A pilot and an engineer from the Test Pilot School at Edwards AFB showed up one day. They had their final assignment in the school. They were to fly the F-105G on three missions to the Tonopah Tactical Range and write a report on the aircraft's suitability for its assigned mission.

They had never seen an F-105G before. They flew one orientation flight and three test missions. They then briefed all of the Weasel crews on the results. It was hilarious to us.

They found the F-105G unsuitable in all aspects for the Wild Weasel mission. Its only positive capability was very high speed at low altitude that would allow it to outrun any enemy aircraft. They were amazed how we could do the Weasel mission and do it well with these aircraft.

F-105G

Loose Screw

We sometimes said that our old, war-torn F-105Gs were falling apart. One day, mine took it for real. I was at Cuddeback Range on a bombing training flight.

While on the downwind leg between drops, I noticed a long screw sticking out from the right front of my canopy. It was sticking out more than three inches and wobbling.

Clearly, it was about to fall out. It was directly in front of the right engine intake, so it would go straight into the engine. That screw could destroy my only engine.

I immediately turned toward George and notified the range controller and George tower of my problem. The Supervisor of Flying came up on tower frequency and said to get it home as quickly and gently as possible.

I flew directly to the George pattern and landed as gently as I could. Maintenance had me shut down at the end of the runway to avoid the bouncing while taxiing that might make it fall out. It stayed in, so all worked out safely.

Crispy Radar

I was flying a local training sortie when my radar completely shut down. I recycled switches, but it was dead, so I just left it turned off. Barbara was Chief of Avionics Maintenance at that time.

A while after I landed from this flight, Barbara's NCO In Charge, a Chief Master Sergeant, walked up to her desk and plopped an 18" by 5" by 6" metal box on her desk. There was blue smoke curling out from it, and it smelled like burned wiring.

He said, "Look what your husband did to my aircraft." It was the power supply from my dead radar. Of course, he was just giving her a hard time, but it was typical of the problems we had with the old aircraft. That part probably cost $500 when it was first built, but by then it cost $10,000.

Basically, all F-105 aircraft in the Air Force had been used up in Vietnam. Almost half of those built crashed or were shot down in Vietnam. The rest were covered with patches and had problems nearly every flight. Most of the Weasel electronics wouldn't last an hour.

Red Flag Emergency

Red Flag is a program at Nellis AFB, NV, where fighter and bomber units deploy from their home bases to fly two weeks of realistic combat training missions. There are very realistic AAA gun and missile radar simulators and US aircraft flying as enemy air defense in the target area. Search and Rescue (SAR) forces are also exercised with aircrew members selected and placed into the desert to be rescued.

This was started after an analysis of years of flying into North Vietnam against the most modern air defenses we have faced. The study showed that the highest probability of being shot down was during a pilot's first ten missions. This gets everyone through those ten missions before going into actual combat.

The biggest plus about flying Wild Weasels at George AFB was Red Flag. George AFB was close enough to the Tonopah Range complex for missions from George to be flown from home base without deploying to Nellis. This also meant that we participated in ALL Red Flag exercises that needed Wild Weasel support. In-flight refueling wasn't necessary, but we usually refueled over the Grand Canyon with the rest of the attack force as part of the exercise.

On rare occasions, our F-105s were tasked to bomb a target instead of as Weasels. This story is about one of those.

I was number 4 in a 4-ship of F-105Gs assigned to each hit a target with 6 inert Mk-82 bombs. All of us were excited for this rare opportunity. The planning and briefing was normal since we didn't have anyone who was new at this. Some of our friends were tasked to be the Weasels providing defense suppression for us. A deployed F-106 unit was tasked as aggressor air for this event. An F-4E unit was our escort for protection from the F-106s.

Our route after departing the KC-135 tanker was north along the east side of the range complex until past Area 51, then west to the target area. We planned to run north in a spread formation at 600 knots. After the turn to west, we would zoom climb to 18,000 feet to get the target in sight and roll in to the left for a 45 degree dive bomb attack. I was on the right end of the formation with everyone spread 500 feet apart.

Just as we turned left to start the climb, an aggressor F-106 came toward me from my right rear on an intercept. Before I could react to the intercept, a red warning light illuminated on my instrument panel. For just a second, I thought the F-106 had actually fired live ammo!

It was a bleed air duct overheat light. The bleed air duct is a 4-inch diameter duct that carries extremely hot, high pressure air from the last stage of the compressor in the engine along the right side of the cockpit to an air turbine just forward of the pilot's right foot. This turbine powers the AC generator and the utility hydraulic pump.

The light is turned on when a sensor wire along the duct senses very hot conditions, meaning a leak in the duct. This can lead to a major fire within seconds, so the immediate procedure is to use the emergency air duct switch to shut off the air flow.

That leaves you with a very basic aircraft. No cabin pressure. No air conditioning. No AC electric power. No hydraulics for lowering landing gear normally. Only a few minutes of battery power to run a radio. You have to slow down to below 250 knots and stay below 10,000 feet.

I declared an emergency, turned toward George AFB, slowed down, and leveled at 10,000, immediately losing sight of the rest of my flight. Lead acknowledged my emergency call. Since I was already headed toward George for the short trip there, no one could catch me before getting there, so he continued to the target with the other two Thuds.

As I slowed, an F-106 being chased by an F-4 came from my left and low and pulled up into a loop around me.

I then saw one of the most amazing sights of my flying career. To my left and going the opposite direction, there was an F-105G in a 45 degree dive just releasing his bombs, an F-106 behind him trying to get a gun camera shot, an F-4 behind the F-106 trying to get a shot of the F-106, and another F-105G in his bomb dive, all lined up in a 45 degree dive!

I was immediately cleared for a visual approach to George, and other traffic was cleared from my path. The flaps are DC electric, so they lowered normally. Emergency gear lowering worked fine. I lined up with the runway for a normal landing at about 200 knots. Touchdown was perfect and I popped the drag chute.

This is where it gets a bit weird. The procedure calls for making a normal landing. However, there is no nose gear steering or normal brakes. Therefore, the next step is to keep the nose up for aerodynamic braking and shut the engine down. Yes, you read that right. There is enough flight control hydraulic pressure from the windmilling engine to keep the nose up. That leaves you rolling down the runway with the nose about 10 degrees up in *total silence*!

Now, you have to steer and stop. The procedure at this point it to reach down by your left knee and pull the emergency brake handle. That releases high pressure fluid from an accumulator tank to make three full brake pedal applications. While still aero braking, I carefully applied brakes and used differential brake pedal pressure to steer. As we slowed, the nose came down and I continued to use brakes to stay on centerline.

It normally takes nearly all of the runway to stop an F-105G. I discovered that, with no engine thrust, it stops less than halfway down the runway. All there was to do now was to sit there and wait for the tug to get into position to hook up.

Unplanned Missing Man Flyover

My squadron had the honor of being chosen to do a flyover at the dedication of the first national veteran's cemetery on the west coast at Riverside, CA. The plan called for a standard 4-ship flight in close fingertip formation to fly over the flagpole at the cemetery as the National Anthem finished. It did not call for number three to pull up and fly out of sight up like missing man is done now.

Due to the poor reliability of our aircraft, we planned eight aircraft to get four to the flyover. We would start up all eight, taxi seven to the runway, and launch six.

I was assigned as number seven. It came time for engine start and mine refused to start. The crew chief tried a few things, but for a reason I never knew, it just wouldn't start.

That's the only time I have ever had an aircraft engine refuse to start. I ended up at the squadron ops desk monitoring the flight on the radio.

The seven remaining Thuds taxied to the runway. As they pulled into the quick check area at the end of the runway, the fight lead had a major hydraulic leak and had to shut down. That left six.

Number three was planned deputy lead, so he took over leading. When they took off, the new leader could not get the landing gear to raise. He was forced to keep flying for a while to burn down fuel weight before landing with questionable landing gear. A fighter with a problem is never left on its own, so number six stayed with him.

There were now four Thuds heading for the cemetery with a flight lead that wasn't planned. Luckily, all Wild Weasel pilots are well qualified flight leads and all knew the plan.

On the way to Riverside, which is only a five-minute flight, number two had a stability augmentation failure. That made his aircraft hard to maintain a good close formation position. It wouldn't be safe for him to participate in the flyover, so he stayed near the point where the flight waited for the radio call to head towards the cemetery. He would rejoin the flight for the trip home.

Then, number three had radio failure. Since he couldn't react to radio calls, the leader (third one) used hand signals to tell him to fly the number two position.

Lead used the radio to tell number two to fly the number four position, leaving the number three position empty.

Finally, the signal came to start the flyover. There were three F-105G aircraft flying as 1,2, & 4. They flew as planned at 350 knots 500 feet over the flag right at the last note of the anthem.

The event was being televised live on all the major networks. The newsman giving live comments said that the Air Force provided a perfect salute for the dedication with a missing man formation. It was a perfect example of teamwork getting the job done.

Barbara and I finally visited that cemetery in 2019. Chief Master Sargent Hopper, who worked for her at George AFB, retired just outside of George and died a few years after that. He is buried in the new cemetery, and we found his grave.

Barbara's Close Call

Towards the end of our tour at George AFB, Barbara was still Chief of Avionics Maintenance. She had about 300 enlisted personnel under her keeping the antiquated electronics working on all the F-4's and F-105's in the six squadrons at George.

One day, we were reminded that AF flying is not only dangerous for the aircrews.

An F-4E was taking off with a student pilot in the front seat and an IP in the back. Shortly after takeoff, while they were still over the runway, the left wingtip folded up.

The F-4 was designed for the Navy, so the outer 3 feet of wing could fold to reduce footprint on aircraft carriers. Navy aircraft had hydraulically folding wingtips that the pilot controlled.

The Air Force left all that extra complexity and weight out and made them manually foldable. When extended, there is a 1-inch diameter red pin that is flush with the surface when the tip is locked down and sticks up about an inch if not locked. The aircrew and crew chief thought it was locked.

When the wingtip folded, the aircraft banked hard left due to the loss of lift on that side. Both pilots pushed the stick and the rudder full right immediately. However, that was only enough to stop the roll at about 90 degrees of bank, not to roll back level.

At this point, they were less than 200 feet above the ramp over rows of F-105G's and sinking. Since they had no way to recover, they did the only thing they could and ejected.

The F-4 continued turning left and rolling, made it past the ramp full of aircraft, crossed just a few feet above the Avionics Maintenance building while inverted, ripped through power lines, and crashed just past the road next to the back gate to the base. It cleared cars on the road by less than 5 feet, just missed a row of parked fuel trucks, and the last burning pieces stopped just short of the large fuel storage tanks.

In the avionics building, Barbara's office was at the corner of the building towards the ramp. Her and others in the office heard a huge roar, and the lights went out.

They ran out the door to find an ejection seat crashing through a van owned by one of their enlisted guys and a pilot landing in his parachute in the parking lot.

The other pilot and seat landed in an open area near the parking lot. The rolling aircraft had passed inverted about 20 feet above Barbara's office according to witnesses.

Barbara always knew that what I did was dangerous, but we now understood that her job was higher risk than we had thought.

Supersonic Below Sea Level

All F-4, F-105, and F-111 pilots train to penetrate defenses by extreme low flying at 100 feet above the ground. F-105 pilots often flew at 50 feet in Vietnam. The only US aircraft that could fly supersonic that low were the F-105 and the F-111.

There was a unique opportunity for Thud flyers at George AFB due to its location between Death Valley National Monument and the Salton Sea. Either place, it was possible to fly supersonic below sea level. Everyone took advantage of this to experience this unique thrill.

Death Valley has very rugged terrain surrounding it with only a small smooth area far enough below sea level to be safe. You can dip down to minus 100 feet momentarily, but it has to be at exactly the right spot to stay 100 feet above the ground. Then, while I was at George, a new Federal Regulation was published that banned supersonic flight over national monuments. That eliminated supersonic flight over Death Valley and dozens of other Air Force training areas.

The Salton Sea, at -235 feet, provides several miles of level water where 100 feet above the water is 135 feet below sea level.

My turn came a day when I was #3 in a 4-ship flight heading for an air-to-air training mission. The air-to-air part was scheduled for the Chocolate Mountain Naval Bombing Range, just east of the Salton Sea. This range is also used for live ordnance deliveries. Both of these area were cleared for supersonic. A training mission like this normally started with a low-level route flown at 100 to 500 feet above ground level.

We planned a route that would take us nearly the full length of the Salton Sea north to south with a 90 degree left turn near the end into Chocolate Mountain Range. We flew a tactical formation spread about 500 feet between aircraft line abreast at 100 feet above the water at about Mach 1.1. That's 680 knots or 780 miles per hour. At the planned point, we made the 90 degree left turn.

As we approached the shore, we were all shocked to see 20 to 30 campers and tents right on our flight path. We couldn't slow down or climb in the few seconds before passing over them. I'm sure that some of them enjoyed the show while others hated us.

When we got back to George, we made some phone calls and found out that it was a new camp ground that just opened the week before. Of course, it wasn't on the maps yet. We passed the word to add it to all maps at George and other Southeast US charts to avoid a repeat incident.

Moved to Command Post

My last year at George was as a Command Post Controller. The Wing Commander was very unhappy with the way the Command Post was operating, and decided he wanted only pilots or WSO's there. It was to be a staff position where you still fly four times per month to maintain minimum proficiency.

They asked for volunteers, so I volunteered to get some visibility due to my junior rank. Just as I started at the Command Post, a decision was made to make the positions non-flying. I think it was mainly due to the lack of aircraft. The operational crews were having a hard time getting enough flights to fill all proficiency training requirements.

An F-4 WSO, two F-4 Pilots, and I were the new Command Post Controllers.

Departure Crashes #9-14

After I stopped flying at George, we lost six F-105 aircraft in six months, two were while I was on duty in the Command Post. Both of those were the same pilot.

The first of those was an F-105G. I was sitting at the Controller console when the crash net activated. The tower controller yelled "A Thud on takeoff ran off the end of the runway. It exploded! It exploded! Roll the trucks!"

They found out later that a tiny spider had built a nest in the pitot tube, which is right on the nose of a Thud. It measures air pressure to calculate airspeed. The spider apparently was so small that it was able to crawl between the tube and the cover that is on it while parked. Its web restricted the airflow and made the airspeed indicator read about 20 knots too high.

The overweight and underpowered Thuds normally used 8 or 9 thousand feet of the 10,000-foot runway to take off. The procedure was to rotate to 10 degrees nose high at 192 knots.

He tried to rotate, but the actual speed was about 172 knots. You really can't feel the difference between those speeds. Applying nose up slab at too low a speed just stalls the slab, and the nose will never come up.

At that speed, and near the end of the runway, he could not get airborne and had no hope of stopping, so he cut the engine and popped the drag chute.

He was far above the speed to successfully use the hook on the cable at the end of the runway. It has ripped Thuds in half trying that. He ran off the end of the runway, then off the end of the 1,000' overrun, then across the perimeter road, and into the desert.

He hit a wood fence at the edge of the base property, causing the right drop tank to explode. A dip in the desert tore all three landing gear off the aircraft. Finally, it slid to a stop on its belly. By then, the right wing was engulfed in flames, and fire was moving toward the cockpit.

The EWO opened the rear canopy, jumped over the left side, and ran about 100 yards away. Electric power to the front canopy motor failed when it was only a few inches open.

Jettisoning the canopy using the pyrotechnics only works if the canopy is closed. The pilot couldn't move it any higher or close it. The EWO saw that the pilot was trapped and ran back to the aircraft. He

135

climbed on top, pulled the emergency T-handle that unlocked the front canopy from its motor, and helped the pilot lift the 300-pound canopy enough to get out. They ran away just as the fire reached the cockpit. The WSO got an Air Medal for this heroism.

The F-105 Director of Operations (DO), Colonel Jim Jones, was acting wing commander. I called him on his portable radio to tell him.

He was driving his staff car near the runway and had seen the whole thing. He was first on scene and was already standing with the air crew.

I also had to call the Wing Commander to report the accident. He was at Bergstrom AFB in the 12th Air Force Commander's office. I had to tell him he had just lost an aircraft while he was in his boss's office. Rough call. It helped that the crew was okay.

The second accident was another F-105G exactly one month later with the *same pilot*. This time, he was returning to base after a routine training mission to the Nellis Range Complex. He was doing a GCA.

About ten miles from landing, the GCA controller lost radar and radio contact. A few seconds later, the crash net activated, and the tower controller said, "We may have a Thud down. GCA lost contact with it, and I see a column of smoke several miles off the approach end of the runway."

I scrambled the fire trucks. A couple of minutes later, Tower came up on the crash net again and said, "An Edwards AFB aero club plane just called and said they saw a Thud crash about ten miles short of the Bergstrom runway. He also said he saw two good chutes." Both crew members had good ejections.

Col Jones was again acting Wing Commander and in his staff car. He could see the smoke and again got to the scene ahead of the fire trucks. When he walked up to the air crew, the pilot pulled off his wings and handed them to him. That close to death twice in a month was too much.

The wing commander was again out of town, so I again had to call to report the accident to him after talking to the DO. My contact board said he was at Tactical Air Command (TAC) headquarters at Langley AFB, VA. I picked up the hot line to TAC Command Post and asked for him. They said he was in the TAC Commander's office. I said, "Patch me through."

The TAC Commander answered the phone. I told him that this was the George AFB Command Post, who I was, and that I needed to talk to the Wing Commander (a Colonel at that time).

He suspiciously said, "O k a y." and handed the phone over. It turned out that the Colonel was briefing the TAC Commander on the results of the investigation of the previous accident! Much rougher call!

They had ejected because the engine quit. The accident board couldn't find anything wrong with the engine.

They did find that when the pilot tried to put the flaps down to land, they wouldn't go down. He followed normal procedure for this and activated the emergency flap system, but that was when the engine quit.

I never saw the official report. However, I do know that the emergency flap switch and the main fuel cutoff switch are right next to each other under the pilot's left elbow. Both have a red cover that is wired shut so that you have to pull hard to break the wire and lift the cover. I'll never know....

Retiring the Thud Weasels

Just before I left this assignment, the F-105G's were being turned over to the Georgia Air National Guard. I think we had 18 flyable aircraft left to hand over and three or four of those were Fs that had never been upgraded to G. Six others might have been flyable if parts could be found.

The F-105s were being replaced at George with the new F-4G Wild Weasel aircraft. F-4Gs were low-time F-4Es with the gun replaced with new electronics added for Weasels. The Georgia crews had been at George AFB for a few weeks training for the Weasel mission in the Thuds.

There were ceremonies when the first four F-105G's went to the Georgia Air National Guard. The George AFB ceremony was a goodbye to the last active duty F-105s. Then, the new squadron commander and three other ANG crews took off for Georgia.

A large group of officials and spectators gathered to welcome them in Georgia. The flight was to be non-stop with two air refuelings. At the first air refueling, one of them couldn't take fuel. It and a wingman diverted to a base in Texas for repair.

The other two made it to Georgia okay. However, the George AFB commander had wanted the aircraft being sent to look perfect. Therefore, he ordered them to be painted two days before the transfer. The paint didn't have time to set fully, and the flight had to pass through an area of rain.

When they landed in Georgia and taxied up to the VIP area with TV and photographers expecting four beautiful aircraft, the paint was gone from wing and tail leading edges and was streaked from the nose all down the sides of the two aircraft.

Uncooperative Assignment System

July 1979

As our three-year tour at George was coming to a close, Barbara and I started negotiating with the Military Personnel Center for our next assignment.

A complication was that we now had a toddler daughter. Also, there were no longer F-105 assignments anywhere, so I had to move to another aircraft. Military Personnel Center started giving me options. They said that I was due for a long tour overseas (three years).

Also, they reneged on the "two-year and then retrain" promise to Barbara. They said that there was a critical shortage of maintenance officers, so she had to take another assignment in that specialty.

Barbara was going to be given an assignment to Germany still as an Avionics Maintenance Officer. At the same time, I would go to Clark AB, Philippines, flying the F-4C interim Weasel aircraft, converting to the F-4G when they were delivered.

Both were 3-year "accompanied" assignments. Unaccompanied assignments were normally 2 years, and remote assignments, such as Korea, were one year. We now had an infant daughter who would have to "accompany" one of us, yet we would be on opposite sides of the Earth for three years!

Military Personnel Center resisted doing joint spouse assignments at that time. The addition of women to the Air Force was just too much for them to figure out, so they were totally uncooperative. We took the 7-day option and chose to separate from the Air Force rather than accept a 3-year separation with an infant.

Transition to Civilians (Temporarily)

August 1979

We both started a job search around southern California.

Barbara completed classes to become a real estate agent. She followed that up by taking a position at Brown Realty in Thousand Oaks. That worked out well when she sold our house when we left there, getting half of the sales cost back.

I decided to do what some of my friends had done and try to get a pilot slot with an airline. To do that, I used the veteran's education plan that pays 90% of school cost to prepare for a new job. I took a course at Orange County (now John Wayne) airport to get an Air Transport Pilot certificate. It was all the academics on civilian aviation rules and procedures plus several hours of flying in a Cessna Citation. It was easy to learn the systems, since they were the same as a T-37.

One of the three guys in my class was a Navy fighter pilot. I was impressed with the way the Citation withstood the "carrier landings." I kept expecting to see the gear struts come up through the wings! Those landings were terrifying for the students in passenger seats.

Since most large aircraft at that time needed two pilots and a flight engineer, I attended a Flight Engineer School in Burbank. Airlines almost always hired their pilots first as an FE, then upgrade to First Officer in a few years. That was two weeks with half of each day in classroom and half flying a Boeing 727 simulator. The class was three students, so we spent each 2-hour session flying one of the three crew positions: Captain, First Officer, or Flight Engineer. Everyone got plenty of landing practice.

After two weeks of that, we went to Denver to take a check flight in an actual 727. We wouldn't be landing the actual plane, just flying as flight engineer. It was a surprise when we found out that we would be flying the first 727 that had been delivered to United Airlines many years earlier. It had a serial number of 006. It looked like it was something from a recycling yard. The interior was stripped of overhead bins and seats except for 5 or 6 seats for students to ride. We would never get to land a 727 at normal operational weights until doing it for an airline. We flew a big triangle between Denver, Boulder, and Colorado Springs for about six hours doing some kind of instrument approach and a touch and go landing at each airport over and over. Pilots getting flight checks to upgrade flew the 727 with us students taking turns at the FE console.

I continued to search and interview for a job. I interviewed with Braniff, but all airlines were in financial trouble at that time and were furloughing pilots instead of hiring.

After several interviews, I was asked by Northrop to take a job managing part of the production line for a new aircraft. That would have used my Purdue degree. It sounded very interesting, They couldn't tell me much about it. It was all close hold stuff. I almost took it, but I wanted to look around more to be sure.

I found a job with Grumman Aircraft Corporation at Naval Air Station (NAS) Point Mugu. It was fine tuning software on the navigation and weapons computers in the F-14. They were very happy to find a fighter pilot who could also do software.

Years later, I discovered that the first aircraft that they wanted me to work on was starting assembly of the F-117 stealth fighter.

Barbara started real estate training and got a sales position with Brown Realty in Thousand Oaks. We sold our Victorville house and bought one in Thousand Oaks. Barbara also started a Masters Degree program at California Lutheran College.

The address of our new house was 2992 Westridge Circle. If you are familiar with aviation, you might recognize that number as the standard day altimeter setting. All pilots set their altimeter to 29.92 inches of mercury, the pressure of a standard day, when above 18,000 feet (12,000 in Europe). The changeover altitude varies slightly in different countries around the world. This assures that all aircraft are at the proper altitude to avoid collisions with aircraft and terrain.

Fate of George AFB

Just as I retired from the Air Force, George AFB closed in 1992 as part of the first Base Realignment and Closure (BRAC) law. The complex is now called the Southern California Logistics Airport.

https://en.wikipedia.org/wiki/Southern_California_Logistics_Airport.

Most buildings have been maintained in the same 2-tone brown coloring that was Air Force standard in the 1980's. They even have the unit names and building numbers from the time of closing.

The housing area and golf course are abandoned and dilapidated. The base hospital where Gwen was born during my time at George in the F-105 was, for several years, boarded up with red signs saying "Asbestos Contamination. Unfit for Human Habitation. Pregnant women should not enter."

Unfortunately, Gwen and Dawn were in the car with us when we visited the old base and discovered this. I drove up to the old hospital while saying, "Gwen, that's where you took your first breath." Oops!

Good news is that the pretty, modern style chapel where Barbara and I were married is now a civilian church.

Grumman Aircraft Corporation

August 1979

The site where I worked was a 3-story building on NAS Point Mugu right at the sea wall overlooking the Pacific Missile Test Range. On the third floor, we had the front end of an F-14 with all skin panels removed. This allowed access to all avionics for attaching test equipment using long cables.

The entire thing was mounted on a pair of rails that ran out through a garage door onto the balcony. The system could be rolled outside where we could turn on the actual radar for testing against airborne targets. It was called the Systems Integration Test Station (SITS).

Here is a link to a 1989 article about the SITS.

https://www.latimes.com/archives/la-xpm-1989-09-14-ve-171-story.html

I was the only pilot in the office, and we did numerous software tests where I flew the SITS. It could be flown just like an F-14 simulator with both cockpits fully functional. I flew it for about 100 hours in each seat. Living in Thousand Oaks, CA, was nice, too.

Working on F-14 software was great. I understood how it was used by the aircrews and could fly it (simulated), so I was an interface between the Grumman engineers and the Navy fight test crews.

While optimizing the computer at the machine code level to reduce memory usage, I discovered an error in the F-14 NATOPS manual. It told the pilots not to use the angle of attack display on the heads-up display (HUD) when the landing gear was down, because it was not accurate.

I ran some tests using the SITS, and all my tests showed it to be accurate. I talked to the Grumman Chief Test Pilot and discovered that this problem only existed in the prototype F-14 and was fixed in all production aircraft. He was surprised that it was still in NATOPS

For some reason, the warning in the NATOPS manual had never been removed. The F-14 pilots were very happy to hear this, because it is much easier to land on an aircraft carrier using the HUD. It allows you to avoid taking your eyes off of the aircraft carrier deck.

I also was able to solve a problem with the Tactical Air Reconnaissance Pod System (TARPS). The test F-14 would take off from Pt. Mugu and fly to NAS Fallon and NAS China Lake out in the Mojave Desert to take photos of test targets. The photos were always blurred. They had been working for several months on the problem.

I went through the code and found the problem within a few minutes. The programmers did not realize that atmospheric conditions are usually different between the takeoff point and the target area. This was especially evident when taking off from sea level at the coast and taking the photos in the high desert.

The existing procedure had the pilot enter correct pressure altitude before takeoff. This told the computer the exact aircraft altitude before takeoff. This was then factored in to system altitude calculations. However, that was never changed in flight to account for different pressure altitude in the target area. This caused the distance the aircraft was above the ground to be calculated wrong.

There was a prism in front of the lens that had to rotate at just the right speed to keep the camera looking at the same spot while the shutter was open. The bad altitude caused the required rotation rate to be miscalculated, causing blurred photos.

I developed a way for the pilot to get more accurate information initially and three ways for the pilot to make the proper correction during flight. The very next test flight produced perfect photos. The Navy was ecstatic to finally have their new photo pod. It was heavily used in DESERT STORM and other contingencies over the next several years.

Saved a Civilian During a Test

Grumman had proposed mounting a steerable camera with a zoom lens in the nose of the F-14 to use for identifying aircraft beyond human visual range. It could be cued by the radar to look at an aircraft the pilot couldn't yet see well.

We mounted it to the SITS and tested it. One test was to have the system automatically track a target. We looked across the water for a good test target and spotted several small sailboats with bright white triangular sails. We locked the camera onto the top of the sail of a boat to test the tracking. It worked as designed.

One of the engineers said to zoom in to the boat so he could get a better look. When we did, all of us saw what he had spotted. There appeared to be only one person in the boat, and he was slumped unconscious over the wheel.

One of our guys called the Pt. Mugu control tower. The controller contacted the Coast Guard. They launched a rescue helicopter.

Of course, there were many small sail boats every day in that area, so the rescue crew didn't know which one to head for. Our guy in the F-14 cockpit could see the boat on the cockpit display and the chopper visually, so he gave directions to the tower to pass to the chopper.

That quickly got it headed for the correct boat. As he approached the boat, the chopper pilot asked where the guy giving directions was located. The camera system was not yet public information, so all he could say was, "I can't say." The tower controller knew not to say, also.

When the chopper got to the boat, they lowered a man to the boat to assist. The man was still unconscious, so they lowered a basket and lifted him into the chopper. They left the rescue man on the boat so he could sail it to shore. We never heard how the guy in the boat was.

Sad Time at Grumman Job

I worked closely with two other software engineers at Grumman. We got along wonderfully and became good friends. Toward the end of my year there, we were running some tests that required 24-hour monitoring. I worked 12-hour day shift, and the other two worked 12-hour night shift.

Around midnight one day, the older one of the two guys went to his car for his 30-minute lunch break. He would normally sit in his car and listen to music on the radio while eating.

This night, he didn't return after 30 minutes. After a while, the other guy went out to the car to check on him. He had died of a heart attack in the car.

California National Guard C-130 Squadron

July 1980

I decided to continue flying by joining the California Air National Guard. I applied and was accepted by a C-130 unit at Van Nuys Airport.

It was the only C-130 unit that had a secondary mission of carrying a fire fighting kit that could dump fire suppressant on forest fires. They figured that an experienced fighter pilot would be an asset for them.

I started flying the simulator that they had and reading the manuals while waiting for a slot in a C-130 training class.

Second Try at the Air Force

August 1980

Barbara and I started getting letters and phone calls asking us to consider returning to active duty. It seems that there was now a critical shortage of fighter pilots in addition to maintenance officers. After a few months of this, we asked how it would work.

They were holding a board similar to a promotion board to consider volunteers for return to active duty. Those selected would then work out an assignment with the Military Personnel Center (MPC). Signing the acceptance for the agreed assignment would be the act that committed them to return.

We decided that there was nothing to lose by trying, so we applied. The board selected less than half of the volunteers and selected both of us.

Getting the assignment was tricky. I was told I had to go to an aircraft I had flown before. Barbara was told she had to go back to maintenance. Training us into some new job was not to be allowed.

However, F-105's and O-2's were no longer used by the Air Force, and no slots in F-4 retraining would be available for a year. I said then I would have to go to an aircraft I hadn't flown before.

We demanded that Barbara would finally get to cross train to Intelligence as was promised years earlier. We also said we wanted to get our long overseas tours together as our first assignments.

We were offered an assignment in Germany with me flying the F-4 and Barbara in Maintenance at a base eight miles away. It would be delayed a year until a training slot was available in F-4 school. We thanked them for trying, but turned those down. It must be much sooner than a year, and Barbara had to move to Intelligence.

A couple of weeks later, we got a call from MPC. They said, "How about a 3-year assignment to RAF Lakenheath, England, with Chuck flying the F-111F and Barbara in Operations Intelligence? Both would be preceded by four months of training in your new jobs."

We accepted quickly before they could change their mind. Needless to say, the C-130 folks were very unhappy with me.

I was only at Grumman for a year, but when I gave my two weeks' notice, my office manager demanded that Personnel provide a replacement who was a fighter pilot who knows software. They didn't think that would be likely. Then, two days before I left, my replacement showed up. He was a previous Navy A-7 pilot and computer programmer! I had him all up to speed easily before I left.

Canon AFB, New Mexico

https://en.wikipedia.org/wiki/Cannon_Air_Force_Base

October 1980

F-111D

I attended F-111 transition training at Canon AFB, NM. The AF only had F-111s at five bases. Each base had a different model. Strategic Air Command had an FB-111 squadron at Plattsburgh AFB, NY. Tactical Air Command had a wing of F-111As at Mountain Home AFB, ID, and a wing of F-111Ds at Cannon AFB, NM. USAF Europe had a wing of F-111Es at RAF Upper Heyford, England, and a wing of F-111Fs at RAF Lakenheath, England.

Arrival Crash #9

Shortly before our arrival, there was an F-111D crash. They had lost an engine and were attempting to land at Canon AFB single engine.

The D was heavy and underpowered and could barely fly on one engine. As they slowed to landing speed within a couple of miles of the runway, they got too slow and started descending too fast. They ejected in time before it crashed.

However, the ejection system didn't work right. The F-111 has a cockpit that doubles as an escape capsule. The entire cockpit with the two crewmembers is rocketed away. It has a large parachute that lets the entire capsule down fairly softly. It also functions as a lifeboat if you land in water.

In this case, maintenance had installed it improperly. Someone had misrouted the main parachute harness to where it tangled, and the chute never opened. They hit the ground at 140 knots and tumbled several times. Both were killed.

Night Automatic Terrain Following in the mountains

The Automatic Terrain Following (ATF) system in the F-111 made it a fantastic aircraft for night bombing. Two capabilities are the most important for bombing targets: penetrating defenses successfully and accurate weapons delivery. At that time, penetrating defenses required "Low and Fast."

Many aircraft and crews have been lost training for this mission.

At night, the lack of visibility requires flying higher than daytime to avoid hitting hazards or the ground. This moves the aircraft up several hundred feet, making it easier to see on radar and giving the defenses more time to coordinate and engage with missiles. The F-111 could maintain the "Low and Fast" technique at night and in most bad weather.

Enemy fighters could try to intercept the F-111, but it was very difficult. The late detection did not give the fighters time to set up an optimum intercept. Once the F-111 got past the fighter, it was free. No fighter at that time could catch a 700-knot F-111 from behind. Our F-111F models at RAF Lakenheath could easily go supersonic at minimum altitude, so only threats ahead mattered, and they had very little reaction time.

Getting down to the low-level run is also automatic. First, we would be level at a medium or high altitude cruise at whatever cruise speed we were using, and the WSO would set up the navigation system for our route. We would run system checks to make sure the TF system was working properly.

Then, we would set the TF to 1,000' and engage it. The aircraft would nose over to about a 10 degree dive. The pilot would adjust the throttles to hold the planned speed.

In front of the pilot was a four-inch round radar screen that showed what the two TF radars were seeing. This was overlaid over the attitude and heading symbology on a large cathode ray tube screen in the F-111D model. The pilot could select either left or right TF as primary. If the one controlling detected a system failure, it would instantly turn over control to the other TF. The pilot would confirm this and do it manually if the automatic system did not do the turnover.

The pilot would monitor these screens continuously while on auto TF. His right hand would hover just in front of the control stick between his legs. There was a paddle switch on the front of the stick that would disconnect the auto TF instantly if squeezed.

Approaching the selected altitude above ground level, the aircraft would level itself at 1,000' above ground level. We would confirm that everything was working properly and start stepping the altitude down. We could select 700', 500', 300', or 200'. For best radar screening, it would always be the lowest setting of 200'.

The WSO watched on the main radar to assure that the autopilot was following the proper course. The course could also be followed manually by the WSO giving verbal steering commands to the pilot.

The WSO also operated the radar jammers and set up the weapons for the attack. Most F-111 missions consisted of the WSO guiding the aircraft using radar imaging of the route and the target area. The weapon would be released at a computer calculated point. Of course, we practiced manual bombing often in case the automatic system failed enroute. Unfortunately, that was quite often.

At Cannon AFB, NM, in the F-111D, I had my first training to use this capability. The low-level routes that we used went through the edge of the Rocky Mountains. Our first night training mission was on the instructor's favorite route.

This route went through one canyon that was only 200-300 feet wide. It passed within 100 feet of the walls in a few places. The unnerving part of this was that regulations required us to run with our red rotating beacon on top of our aircraft turned on for safety in case another aircraft was nearby.

It would be totally black outside with no ground lights at all in the mountains. The auto TF system was smart enough that it ignored any terrain that would miss the wingtips by at least 40 feet. At the points where we passed close to the canyon wall, the rotating beacon would suddenly illuminate the wall in bright red light. It was impossible to not jump at each of these glimpses of rock level with our heads right next to us.

Night low-level in England, Scotland, and France was much more relaxing with mostly flat farmland.

One other quirk of auto TF was weather that included heavy rain. The TF radars would be working perfectly while passing through fog, clouds, or rain. But if you approached a classic "wall of rain", the TF radar thought it saw a solid mountain and tried to climb over it. The pilot had to take over manually and fly a safe altitude until out of the rain.

If I had to penetrate the modern defenses of Russia, China, or any other adversary during those Cold War years, the F-111F was the aircraft I would choose.

F-111D More than Maintenance Could Handle

The F-111D had state-of-the-art electronics including flat panel computer screens instead of separate round instruments. Actually, the electronics were pushing the state of the art a bit too much. The result of that is always unreliability.

The in-commission rate of the F-111D was terrible. We double-scheduled. You had to be on the schedule twice to be likely to fly once. Maintenance was taking constant shortcuts and skipping much of the documentation paperwork in their attempt to keep the planes flying.

Once, I was walking out to the assigned aircraft with a student WSO and the crew chief when I suddenly stopped dead. The other two stopped and ask what was wrong. I said, "Do you see anything unusual?" They looked at the aircraft and one said, "Oh my God!"

There was no trailing edge flap on the left wing. That's about a 12' by 3' piece of wing missing. It had been removed for some reason but not recorded in the maintenance record.

Another time, I started to climb into the cockpit when I noticed that neither control stick was there. Again, parts had been used to fix another aircraft without recording it.

This was officially called "cannibalizing," "canning" for short. It was a standard procedure, but had to be approved and carefully documented.

Finally, TAC sent an inspection team with no notice and went through the entire maintenance organization. It was a mess. There were even dozens of critical parts sitting on shelves with no record that they were there. Many aircraft were parked for weeks waiting for parts that were right there all along.

The Maintenance Commander, the Logistics Commander, and a few others were fired. I never saw the end results, but they all had enough years to retire. Reliability of the aircraft was starting to get much better just as I left.

Barbara's Retraining

Barbara went to Lowry AFB, CO, near Denver, for Intelligence Officer training. We had Gwen, our 2-year old daughter to plan around. We decided for Gwen to go with Barbara since she would be in an academic situation, while I would be in flight training with varying day and night schedules.

Barbara arranged for Gwen to stay at the Lowry AFB Day Care Center each day while she was in class.

We bought a new condo in Aurora for Barbara and Gwen to live for the four months. The plan was to rent it out while we were in England and sell it upon return, hoping to gain value on it.

Half way through the four months, I rented a Cessna Cardinal and flew to Denver to visit them for a couple of days. My O-2 time was useful.

After training, we took some leave to visit our home towns, shipped our household goods and two cars, and headed for a foreign country.

Unfortunately, the housing market in Colorado collapsed while we were in England, so we lost a few thousand on the condo. At least they had a comfortable place to live for those four months. Without the condo, we would have had to pay rent.

RAF Lakenheath, England

http://www.lakenheath.af.mil/

Jan 1981

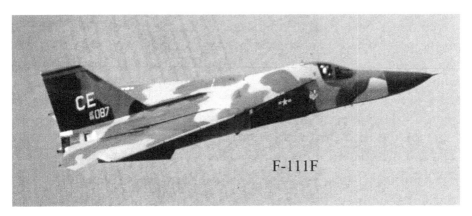

F-111F

Arrival Crash #10

The day before we arrived at Lakenheath, an F-111F crashed near the town of Thetford a few miles from the base and within five miles of where we lived for the next three years. A hydraulic actuator on the tail jammed, making the aircraft uncontrollable. They ejected just before impact, and the chute opened just in time.

Okay. With this history, I don't dare tell any place that I'm coming.

Moving Overseas

An overseas move at this time for us was not simple. Having a 2-year old was tricky, but we handled that part okay. We had to sell the Varieze and some other things, then put most of our other belongings into storage for the next three years. Then, it took two months to get our things delivered in England due to consecutive strikes by the customs employees, the dock workers, and the truck drivers. We shipped two cars, which came through in good shape when we finally got them.

There is a lot involved in moving a family to England. First, you have to learn the language. No kidding! Many words have very different meanings over there.

You don't have to get upset if someone wants to talk to your daughter and says he will "Knock her up this evening." He's just going to knock on the house door.

The first time a guy asked me if I'd like to "have a fag", I didn't know he was offering me a cigarette, so I just walked away.

Of course, you have to learn to drive on the left side of the street. It takes weeks or months to train your eyes and reflexes. I never did get to the point where I automatically used my right hand to turn the turn signals on. If I turned right, I usually signaled by turning on the windshield wipers using the lever on the left of the steering wheel.

I only made a serious mistake once. In London, I was turning left onto a 4-lane street with a median, and I turned into the lanes to the right of the median. Luckily, there weren't any cars coming, and I realized the mistake immediately. There was a driveway handy to turn around.

Second Daughter

The highlight of this assignment was the birth of Dawn, our second daughter, six months after arriving in England. That actually makes her both a US and a British citizen by birth. Unfortunately, it means that she initially had to prove her USA citizenship by showing both her British birth certificate and her "Report of Birth Abroad" certificate. Once she had a passport, it became acceptable identification.

We had a couple of years to establish a routine before starting our older daughter in school. Of course, we did have to arrange "child minders" for times where we were both pulled away by AF duties.

F-111F

There were several models of the F-111 built. The F was the last. The main difference was that its engines had 50% more thrust. That's like hanging a third engine on it! That gave it a takeoff roll about 40% shorter than the other models. It was so efficient that it could either use a lot less fuel than the others and go farther, or it could cruise a lot faster.

I was used to the F-105 being the fastest plane in the world at low altitude. Now, they were retired, and the F-111F was even faster. No one could ever catch it from behind. It could reach Mach 1.2 or 1.3 at near sea level. The aircraft did not have a stated maximum speed. It had a skin temperature limit. You could push it as fast as you want as long as the skin temperature warning does not light up.

152

We could cruise at 200 feet above the ground on automatic terrain following (ATF) and run through enemy territory at 670 knots or more day or night even in bad weather. That speed even allowed the wingman plenty of extra speed for maneuvering in formation. We could actually push it to the upper 700's, getting supersonic at very low altitude. This makes it VERY difficult for defenses to react in time to get a shot at it. It was the best aircraft the US had for penetrating heavy defenses. Finally we could go low and fast in any weather any time of day!

One strange thing was that, in the F-111, we almost never flew 4-ship flights. That was because the cockpit seated the pilot and WSO side-by-side with a solid wall behind them. The cockpit was also wide. The result was that the pilot couldn't see number four if the element was on the right side. This made 4-ship formations difficult and added unnecessary risk. So, we flew 2-ship or 3-ship flights most of the time. Actual combat missions would usually be planned for 2-ship or single-ship.

The F-111F pushed the state of the art to the very edge, reducing reliability. The engines and airframe were pretty reliable, but the avionics were terrible. Mean Time Between Failure (MTBF) was 30 minutes. Our normal training sorties were 3 hours, 4 or more if air refueling.

Combat sorties can be much longer. Consider that MBTF when you realize that the attack on Libya (which occurred a year after I left) was a 13-hour mission. We practiced a lot for manual operation, since the automatic stuff wasn't reliable. I always said that, if everything was working, the pilot's job was to get the WSO airborne and back on the ground.

Barbara was finally an Intelligence Officer. She spent most of our time at Lakenheath as Assistant Chief of Operations Intelligence. This made her responsible for keeping informed on all enemy threats to our operations and keeping the aircrews informed. So, she knew exactly what defenses we were up against with the Warsaw Pact. That's not exactly comfortable knowledge for a pilot's wife, especially because estimates on capabilities of our adversary's air defense systems tended to give them better capability than they really had.

Lightning Pinball with A-7s

RAF Sculthorpe, about 40 miles northeast of Lakenheath, did not have a permanent aircraft organization stationed there. It was in standby status with an RAF Base Commander and 13 USAF personnel living there with their families.

It would occasionally host a small contingent of US aircraft for an exercise. In 1983, we activated it for six months while the Lakenheath runway was rebuilt. We moved all flyable F-111s from Lakenheath to Sculthorpe for the duration. We also opened the maintenance facilities and moved many personnel into barracks there temporarily.

As Assistant Chief of Operations Plans, I was responsible for planning for our F-111F operations while at Sculthorpe.

During this time, a contingent of five US Air National Guard A-7s deployed to Sculthorpe for a two-week exercise. These were some of the same A-7s that had replaced my F-4 squadron in Thailand.

When they were scheduled to arrive, I was part of a welcoming group that included all RAF Lakenheath senior officers, local British officials, and even the area Member of Parliament.

The A-7s flew across the Atlantic non-stop along with KC-135 tankers to keep them fueled. They had been airborne for about seven hours. The tankers landed at an active RAF Base that has a squadron of USAF KC-135s already based there.

The A-7s lined up in a 5-ship right echelon formation to fly over the runway before landing. A flying aircraft can build up a significant electrical charge, especially in humid conditions.

Just as they passed directly in front of the welcoming crowd, there was a blinding flash. All the A-7s wobbled around and started breaking out of formation, Pieces of metal and other things fell onto and along the runway.

There was a very small black cloud, not more than 200 feet wide, that sent a huge bolt of lightning into the tail of number 5 and from there though the other 4 aircraft. The largest part that fell was the top half of number 5's rudder. The lightning fried some of the electronics in all five A-7s and destroyed the Pave Penny laser sensor pods they were carrying.

The aircraft circled the field a while looking each other over and checking out controls and everything they needed to land safely. While they were doing this, all of us on the ground, including VIPs, ran to the runway and cleared the bits and pieces off of it so they could land.

When they landed, the RAF Base Commander shook the A-7 Commander's hand and said, "Welcome to Great Britain." Everyone laughed, partly out of relief that there hadn't been a major accident. The maintenance crews worked 24-7 and managed to get the A-7s

154

operational one by one. They were able to fly most of the exercise sorties that were scheduled.

F-111F Takeoff Abort

Due to the poor reliability of the F-111F, emergencies were common. On takeoff on one flight, I had lifted off and was reaching for the landing gear handle still at max power when the Main Fuel Pump Failure warning light came on. According to the manual, that meant flame out on both engines within two seconds. It's one of those "I hope I never see it." lights.

We were 30 or so feet in the air, so I yanked the throttles to idle, left the gear down, and held a landing attitude. I keyed the mike and said "Main fuel pump failure! Aborting!"

I expected to lose both engines at any second even with the throttles at idle. I started wondering how hard the flame-out landing would be. To my surprise, I made a normal landing and taxied to the end of the runway and off onto the inspection ramp with the engines still running.

It turned out that the problem was a pressure sensor that failed, lighting the pump failure light. This would have been a disaster in the F-4 or F-105 due to running out of runway. However, the F-111F takes off in only 2,400 feet. With 6,000 feet of runway still in front of me, the landing was routine. This was my second 0.1 hour flight, but this time I logged a landing, too.

Deployment to Aviano AB, Italy

For training in the Mediterranean area, we deployed my entire squadron (18 aircraft) to Aviano AB, Italy, for a month. There was a bombing range in northern Italy that we could use. We were able to plan low-level routes throughout most of Italy and Switzerland and over the seas around Italy.

The short route there from England is, of course, across France. However, the French at that time were very uncooperative with the US military. We planned the normal route across France which would get us there in an hour and a half. Since we expected problems, we had a backup plan.

We filed the flight plan 24 hours ahead as per French requirements, and confirmed it the morning of the flight. We formed into 3-ship flights and departed RAF Lakenheath about 30 minutes apart. My flight was the first. I was number 2.

When we reached the point over the English Channel where we would enter French airspace, Lead called for permission. The French controller said, "Standby." He expected us to orbit in English airspace until he cleared us. This trick is often pulled by the French. They sometimes refuse permission until the US aircraft no longer have enough fuel to make it to their destination, so they have to turn back. I don't think they realized that our F-111s have three times the range of most other fighters.

It was time to use our backup plan. We all turned our radar transponders off to avoid being seen by Air Traffic Control. Lead and 3 went to one of our tactical radio frequencies. I stayed on the French Air Traffic Control frequency. We then turned west and proceeded on our backup plan route. We flew down the English Channel to the Atlantic Ocean. Then, we turned south and stayed in international airspace down the coast of France. Lead contacted Spanish controllers who immediately granted clearance to cross the northern neck of Spain to Italy.

Meanwhile, I called the French controller every 3 or 4 minutes requesting our clearance. They always answered "Standby." Finally, just as we were getting to Italy, I received clearance to cross France. I answered, "Thanks anyway, but it's too late, now." They probably celebrated ruining another USAF mission. We landed at Aviano AB a few minutes late, but had a much more interesting flight. The flights behind us got the standby trick, too, but none of them had to wait so long for clearance.

Alpine Terrain Following

At Aviano, we flew several low-level routes through the Alps and used the Italian bombing range for two weeks. That was some spectacular low-level flying! The routes wound through mountain valleys and between peaks. Two of the peaks were only about 300 feet apart. Many of the routes were in unpopulated areas where we could cruise at 600 knots at 200 feet.

One of the routes went through a valley with a large cable car system that went up the north side of the valley. This was the cable car system that, 17 years later in 1998, had an EA-6B fly through the cable, killing the ten people in the car and damaging the aircraft. We manually updated all of our charts before deploying, so this cable and several others was properly notated on our chart. We planned our route 1,000 feet above each cable.

Saved a TSGT

During this deployment, some maintenance personnel were being given right seat rides. One Technical Sergeant, a guy in his thirties, was about to take a ride. Our Flight Surgeon was giving quick checkups to everyone before their ride.

He went into a small briefing room to check the guy out. Less than two minutes later, he came running out of the room yelling, "*Call an ambulance*!"

I was standing there and grabbed a phone, but someone else was faster on the phone.

I asked what was wrong. The doc said the guy's heart rate was over 250 and he was within minutes of a massive coronary.

They got an AF ambulance, we loaded him in, and they took him to an Italian heart center at Vicenza. He was on the operating table surrounded by Italian and USAF doctors immediately.

They ended up doing a triple bypass and saved him. Luckily, he had over 20 years in the AF, so he could retire on disability immediately.

Our last two weeks there, an incredible thick fog settled in. We never even started an engine for that two weeks. Visibility was about 100 yards most of the time.

Several of us went every day to the 9-hole golf course on base, rented clubs, bought balls, and played golf. We lost a lot of balls in the fog.

While we were there, the golf course opened a shop and stocked Ping clubs. I needed a new set to replace my old high school clubs, and the price was half the normal price. I bought a full set, and it came in a nice bag. I still have those clubs.

The fog cleared just in time for us to fly back to RAF Lakenheath on schedule. When traveling like this in an F-111, we would put luggage into the empty weapons bay and tie it down. That's how my clubs made it back to England.

Wrong Ships in Target Area

Back at RAF Lakenheath, we got back to normal daily training. I was leading a 3-ship flight scheduled for training against US Navy ships. We were given a point in the Atlantic Ocean about 200 miles southwest of Ireland. The ships were to be within a 25 nautical mile

(NM) radius around that point. The ships were a heavy cruiser, a smaller guided missile cruiser, and a destroyer.

For training missions like this, we would practice a missile or laser guided bomb attack on the ships and they would practice detecting incoming aircraft and tracking us with their missile guidance radars.

We headed out to sea southwest of Ireland towards the target area with two and three spread a mile on each side of me. We immediately went to our 200-foot Automatic Terrain Following (ATF) setting to get under their radars and pushed our speed up to 670 knots. We used our radars to look for the ships. At nine miles per minute, we got into the target area fast.

We went directly through the area north to south but didn't find any ships. I decided to make a pass back through the eastern part of the circle at 500 feet to get a better radar look. Still, there were no ships, and we didn't detect any of their radars.

We were now a bit frustrated. I thought the ships might be running a little behind schedule and decided to make a north to south pass through the western part of the circle again starting at 500 feet so we could "see" farther.

As we entered the area, we picked up three ships on radar, one large, one small, and one midsized, moving west to east just inside the circle. Yes, they *were* running late! I called for descent to 200 feet and pushed back up to 670 knots.

As we got closer, we turned off the ATF and descended manually to 100 feet for the final run. I took the largest ship and assigned the others to two and three. We pushed our speed up to 700 knots, barely subsonic. Each of us aimed to pass just off the bow of our target ship.

As we passed the ships, I was shocked at what I saw. I yelled to my WSO, "Did you see what I saw?" He responded, "Yeah. The deck was *red*."

Two and three noticed it, too. I led the flight northeast toward Ireland low and fast for a while. You see, only one country paints the decks of their warships red – Russia! Clearly, we caught them completely by surprise, because they never turned on their radars. They missed a great training opportunity.

As soon as we returned to RAF Lakenheath, we called the Navy command center. They said that, as the US ships were approaching the area, they spotted the Russian ships heading for the same place. To avoid an incident, the US ships stayed well west of the area, so we never saw them. At our low altitude, no one could reach us by radio from England.

There were no reports from the Russians complaining about us buzzing their ships. I'm sure they enjoyed that as much as the US sailors always do. When we do a ship attack, there are always hundreds of sailors on the deck with cameras. I wonder if any Russians got good F-111 photos.

Chuck and Barb Show

During our last year at RAF Lakenheath, I was assigned as Assistant Chief of Wing Plans and Barbara was the Chief, Intelligence Operations Branch. During exercises and emergencies, we both worked the 12-hour night shift at the command post. Our F-111F wing was heavily scheduled for night attack using our Pave Tac Pods with IR camera and LASER illumination capability. We had an arrangement with a British neighbor to drop our daughters off with them at any time on no notice. It worked well several times.

I worked in the "Battle Cab" with the Big 4: the Wing, Base, Maintenance, and Logistics Commanders. This "Cab" was an elevated, glassed-in observation room overlooking the entire Command Post. I was responsible for writing the Wing Commander's checklist and monitoring use of it during exercises or war if I wasn't scheduled to fly.

During exercises, there would be extra missions tasked. These were usually single-ship missions that weren't on the planned schedule. We would have 20 minutes from receipt of the tasking message to plan. I worked the operations plan for a crew, aircraft, weapons, and flight plan.

Barbara was in charge of night shift in the Intel shop right next to the Battle Cab. She worked the intelligence situation on the target and defenses. At the end of that 20 minutes, we had to brief the Battle Staff. We would set up a briefing board and wall map in the Intel shop. The Wing Commander, Col Ed Bracken, would look over at Barbara and I and say, "Is the Chuck and Barb show ready?" We made a great team.

Dual-Base Air Show

The 48th Tactical Fighter Wing at Lakenheath was known as the "Stature of Liberty Wing." In the center of a traffic circle in front of Wing Headquarters, was a six-foot statue made from one of the actual molds used to design the Stature of Liberty. It was presented by France July 4, 1954, to symbolize US-French friendship. Every year during the week of July 4, RAF Lakenheath hosted a carnival and invited the public to attend for free. Ironically, I am writing this on July 4, 2020.

During my last year there, the Wing Commander, Col Ed Bracken, decided to add an air show to the carnival. Since I was Assistant Chief of Wing Plans, I was tasked to arrange the whole event, carnival and air show. Luckily, we had a major who had run an air show before.

Getting the carnival set up required power and water for their caravan park. I had to arrange contracts with the British electricians union to plug in a long extension cord, the plumbers union to screw a hose onto the water outlet, the carpenters union to put two boards across the street to protect the cord and hose, and both plumbers and carpenters to attach the cord and a faucet on a stake at the camp. Unions control every little thing England.

The air show worked out very well. We had numerous military planes from several countries on static display. The flying show include demonstrations by several single historic and modern planes and two groups.

We arranged a flyby of four F-111Fs demonstrating the variable wing sweep. They flew in close trail formation with wings at 72 degrees for lead, 45 for two, 26 for three, and 16 for 4. Another F-111F approached the runway in landing configuration, lit the afterburners, raised the gear and flaps, started sweeping the wings back, accelerated to about 400 knots, and pulled into an almost vertical climb until he was out of sight, a great demonstration of its power.

What made this show truly unique is that we flew it over two bases on the same flights. RAF Chicksands is a mostly US manned base about 50 miles SE of Lakenheath, but is not an air base with a runway. All participating aircraft would take off from Lakenheath and do their routine, then fly to Chicksands to do the routine there while the next participant flew over Lakenheath, then land back at Lakenheath.

It all went very smoothly with unusually good weather as a great show of airpower. Of course, the British always love an air show.

Embry Riddle Aeronautical University

Yes, I know that Embry Riddle is in Florida. However, every evening at Lakenheath, the DoD Dependents High School became ERAU. Several USAF members were qualified instructors for several ERAU courses. The schedule was arrange so that anybody who arrived on a 3-year tour could complete a Masters degree in either Aeronautical Science or Airport Management. I did Aeronautical Science.

Anti-Nuke Demonstrations

During much of our tour at Lakenheath, anti-nuclear protests were spreading throughout Europe. A group often decided to try to keep Lakenheath personnel from getting into the base in the morning. We would approach the main gate and find dozens of protesters carrying signs and standing in the road. My favorite sign was "Hell no. We won't glow!"

What really angered me was that there would be children laying in the street right outside the gate. The Security Police could drag adults out of the way, but they had to carefully pick up each child and place them the other side of the street. A few minutes later, an adult would walk them back and show them where to lay.

The thing is, these weren't their children! They "rented" the kids for the day. They would go to houses where people who needed money lived, and pay them for using their child. Does that make that child an employee or a slave?

Departure Crashes #15-20

Assistant Chief of Operations Plans was a non-flying job, so I was no longer flying my last year at Lakenheath. Again, we did not lose an aircraft during the time I was actively flying there. However, the last 6 months I was there, we lost one aircraft each month. On 2 of those, the crew was killed. My record of no aircraft losses while I was actively flying with a Squadron, but losses just as I arrived and after I quit flying was disastrous.

Fort Hood, Texas

http://www.hood.army.mil/

Feb 1984

TACP Jeep & trailer

TACP Hummer

Moving back from England

When we got our stored household goods back after three years of storage at Port Hueneme, CA, there were problems. We had stored an aluminum 6-foot step ladder. They delivered a beat-up 5-foot wooden ladder. The top was ripped off our Kimble Crest piano. A Civil War shotgun that had been given to me by my landlord at Purdue was stolen. At least none of our furniture seemed to have been rented out like happened to other military families. Insurance paid me $100 for the shotgun that had been found on a Civil War battlefield.

Since our previous homes had been in California, everything in Texas seemed very inexpensive. We bought a very nice one-story house in Killeen, TX, with a big swimming pool in the back yard and a golf course two blocks away. right outside of Fort Hood. We became the entertainment center for my AF Detachment with pool parties most weeks in good weather.

Arrival Crash #11

My first week there, one of our enlisted men was killed when he rolled a jeep on a rugged tank trail. Here we go again!

Barbara Goes Reserve

Barbara's assignment was with an evaluation and test unit at West Fort Hood. She worked several exercises evaluating coordination between the Army and Air Force.

After two years, she decided to leave active duty and join the Air Force Ready Reserve as an Individual Augmentee. She drove to NAS Dallas once each month for weekend training.

Welcome to the 2nd Armored Division

I was the Air Liaison Officer (ALO) for 2nd Brigade, 2nd Armored Division, 3rd Corp. This brigade was called the "St. Lo Brigade." The army names brigades after their most important battle, usually one where nearly everyone was killed. This brigade had made the first breakout from the D-Day beachhead during WWII at St. Lo, France, and lost about 90% of its troops doing it.

Met General Patton

One of the first events after I arrived was a Division Commander change of command ceremony. I asked who the outgoing commander was. The answer was "General George Patton." I said "Riiiiiight."

I had read some division history, and I knew that Gen George Patton formed the division during WWII, road marched it (tanks and all) all the way from Texas to the east coast, loaded it onto ships, offloaded in Africa, and fought the Germans in north Africa. I also knew that he was killed in an auto accident after the war while still in Germany.

This was 1984. It turned out that the outgoing commander was Gen George Patton II, his son. The ceremony with the entire division formed up in front of representative vehicles from each unit in the division was the largest military formation that I have ever seen. There were somewhere around 20,000 of us who marched in formation.

I found out quickly that there was a tradition at 2AD. Fort Hood had an exercise area larger than Rhode Island, so it could handle a division-sized field exercise. 2AD had every January reserved for the entire division to go into the field the entire month every year. I got to do that for 5 Januaries! Of course, this was great training for deploying to Germany to meet the Warsaw Pact forces in European weather.

Five National Training Center (NTC) Rotations

I also "got to go" on five 3-week June or July 1984-88 rotations to the National Training Center at Fort Irwin, CA. That's in the Mojave Desert. That time of year, it's 100 to 130 degrees in the daytime.

We simulated war against the Warsaw Pact, so we operated as if we were under chemical weapon attack during the battles. That meant wearing full chemical defense outfits over our uniforms and a gas mask. The Army uses real CS tear gas for training, so we took it seriously.

I arranged for A-10 and F-16 support for the two weeks of actual maneuver days including live fire attacks.

First NTC Rotation

2nd Brigade was selected to deploy two battalions to NTC my first year there. This was only the second Brigade with the new M-1 Abrams tanks and M-2 Bradley armored personnel carriers (APC) to go to NTC. Apparently, the first brigade to take the new vehicles had not had time to learn their capabilities before deploying, so it did not go well.

There were two battalions of vehicles stored at NTC and used by deploying units. All of this was older types of vehicles, so we had to deploy everything.

We loaded two battalions of M-1 tanks, M-2 APCs, Paladin 155mm artillery guns, and support vehicles onto three long freight trains for the vehicles. That's over 200 vehicles. It took several 747 and DC-10 aircraft for the personnel.

We were lucky when the AF provided a KC-10 for the ALO deployment. We could carry all our vehicles and personnel in one KC-10. Our KC-10 even provided in-flight refueling for some C-141 aircraft that carried high-value Army equipment.

The opposition force (OPFOR) at Ft. Irwin had primarily old US Sheridan tanks that were visually modified to look like either Soviet T-72 tanks or Soviet BMP APCs.

All vehicles and personnel were equipped with the Multiple Integrated Laser Engagement System. (MILES) This consisted of lasers bore-sited with all direct fire weapons and receivers on all potential targets, vehicles and personnel.

The laser was triggered by the sound of a blank round being fired. Therefore, the entire logistics system had to work to get the ammo to wherever it was needed and the weapon had to work.

When a laser hit a receiver, the laser code showed the type of weapon and reported appropriate damage to the target. All of this was transmitted to the central control center, recorded, and displayed in motion on a large screen at the debriefing at the end of each battle.

The OPFOR knew every inch of the exercise area and all the tricks for using the rugged terrain. However, they had not done their homework on the new 2AD capabilities. I think that they expected us to be as bad as the first deployment.

The new 2AD equipment was highly mobile, reliable, and had very accurate day and night sighting systems which even worked on the move. For the first time in its history, the OPFOR lost almost every engagement!

One incident during this rotation was unique. We were in an area that had been an artillery firing range during WWII. The Army spent years clearing unexploded ordnance. It was finally declared cleared and ready for use the previous year.

I was in a bare desert valley and needed a toilet. Of course, there was none. Following proper procedure, I walked a few hundred feet from our vehicle into a small depression. I pulled out my folding shovel and dug a hole. Then I squatted over the hole.

I looked down into the hole and was looking right at the nose fuse of a WWII mortar round!!! I carefully backed away. Then, I marked the area with some yellow tape and reported it to the NTC controllers so that they could get a crew to get rid of it.

I carefully dug a hole at a different location to finish what I was doing. Then, I passed the word that the area wasn't as clear as we were led to believe.

More NTC Rotations

In later rotations, a MILES transmitter was developed that was mounted on the A-10 aircraft. It didn't require a blank round. It worked from the gun trigger and fired instead of the gun.

For the first time, the Army saw the effectiveness of the A-10. When a battle started, the A-10s quickly put nearly all the OPFOR vehicles out of action. When the Army reached the battlefield, all they had to do was pick off a handful of OPFOR vehicles and accept the surrender.

The Army argued that this was ridiculous. We pointed out that we had been telling them for years what the A-10 could do. A few years later in Iraq, DESERT STORM had the same results.

After a couple of days, the Army had to change the rules. The Army units weren't getting any worthwhile training with the AF wiping out the OPFOR. They changed it so that any OPFOR vehicle that was knocked out by an A-10 was only out of action for 15 minutes.

Of course, the A-10 system also had a receiver. If you pointed a hand-held missile, like a Stinger, at it and fired, the A-10 would signal the hit to the pilot and the master score system. However, the Army quickly discovered just how hard it is to point directly at a maneuvering 320-knot target and squeeze a trigger. They rarely got a hit.

Chain of Command

On our third rotation, Army/Air Force relations were strained beyond limits. On each rotation to NTC, the trains for army vehicles were mostly open flat-bed cars with everything chained in place.

The Air Force learned the hard way that, if the ALO jeeps were sent that way, the half-million dollars' worth of radios in each jeep would disappear before getting there. All of the radios were like the ones the Army uses.

To keep the AF equipment secure, we had to use boxcars for our jeeps and trailers and put seals on the box car doors. We loaded and unloaded them ourselves. That took several hours at each end. Wooden chocks must be nailed to the wooden floors and everything must be chained in place.

Two of our enlisted personnel then rode the entire two-day trip in the caboose of the train to guard the jeeps. The rest of us would travel in the transport aircraft with the Army personnel. Perry Smallwood and I were the Brigade ALOs. Two Battalion TACPs were also deployed.

When the exercises were over, we went to load the jeeps, and there were no box cars. The same Army logistics officer who scheduled the train to deploy forgot to schedule the box cars to go home even though they were on our transportation requirements list. It was going to take a week and thousands of dollars to get boxcars and a train to pick them up. To load the box cars, we would have to fly our guys to California and back commercially.

Our Tactical Airlift Liaison Officer (TALO) found out that there were three C-141 aircraft scheduled to fly from Norton AFB, CA, to Fort Hood the next day to pick up an Army air defense unit and take them home to Fort Bliss, TX. The C-141s were not scheduled for cargo going to Fort Hood, and Norton AFB is only 60 miles from Fort Irwin. We could drive there in less than two hours. This would get our jeeps back securely the same time as us and save the Army tens of thousands of dollars.

Then, service rivalries between senior officers completely blew up. The Fort Hood Brigade Commander told us "You travelled here with us, and you're going to travel back with us." He insisted that we "belong to him" and would travel on the passenger transports with the Army troops.

We pointed out that we would have to find a secure location for our jeeps for a week, then fly our 14 people back to Fort Irwin to load the jeeps on a train, then fly our people back to Fort Hood. All that plus the train would cost the Army tens of thousands of dollars. He insisted that we were under his command and would follow his orders. That's where he was wrong.

We checked with our AF Detachment Commander at Fort Hood, and he ordered us to take the C-141s. From there, it continued up the chain of command with the Air Force commanders ordering us to get on the C-141s, and the Army commanders ordering us to get on the transports with the Army troops.

Finally, the two-star general NTC commander ordered us to go with the Army or he would have us arrested. The 3-star 12th Air Force commander ordered us to go on the C-141s.

The Air Force Detachment at Fort Irwin had a small compound with a tall chain link fence around it to secure the AF vehicles and offices. We were sleeping on the floor there when not in the field. We told the Army folks that we would be leaving the compound at 0800 the next morning to head for Norton AFB. Then we all went to sleep.

At 0500 the next day, well before sunrise, we quietly headed out from the AF compound in our jeeps without turning on any lights. Instead of heading for the Fort Irwin main gate, we took an obscure dirt tank trail that went through the desert almost to Barstow, halfway to Norton AFB. There, we got onto I-15 to Norton. We arrived at the Norton motor pool wash pits, cleaned our vehicles, and loaded them and ourselves onto the C-141s.

We found out later that the NTC Military Police had surrounded the AF compound at 0730 to arrest us at 0800. By then, we were not far from Norton.

Of course, the Army generals were not happy. The 2AD commander ordered his Judge Advocate office to draw up charges to court martial Perry and I.

Perry and I went to the Air Force Judge Advocate office at Bergstrom AFB to explain the whole situation. The AF lawyers there quickly pulled out documents proving that we, and all ALOs. were always under AF command, and did not have to obey the Army orders. They provided copies to us to take back to Fort Hood and keep at the AF detachment.

The 2AD commander was very unhappy when his JAG office came to the same conclusion and informed him that we were obligated to "obey the rightful orders from senior officers of other services" only if they were in our chain of command. We were within our rights in what we did.

By our fifth rotation, Ft. Irwin finally had M-1 and M-2 vehicles and we had Hummers instead of jeeps, The AF provided a KC-10 for the AF vehicles and personnel, so we no longer needed the trains. Also, the new 2AD Chief of Staff who knew me from the An Loc battle was there, so relations with the Army were the best ever.

New Chief of Staff

At division level, there are two AF Air Liaison Officers (ALO) and one Tactical Airlift Liaison Officers (TALO). The junior ALO is called a Fighter Liaison Officer (FLO), but is really simply a second ALO.

While I was 2AD FLO, a new ALO, Bill, arrived. He had been shot down flying an F-4 over Vietnam and spent over two years as a POW.

About the same time, a new Army Colonel arrived as the new 2AD Chief of Staff (CoS). He wanted to meet his AF support and asked Bill and I to come to his office.

We arrived and introduced ourselves. He asked about our backgrounds. It turned out that he was in Vietnam the same time as us. He asked our most interesting experiences there.

Of course, for Bill it was as POW, which was at the same time that the other two of us were there. I decided, since we were supporting an armored division, I would tell him about An Loc, where I got a tank kill that stopped the tank from firing into the door of the command bunker. When I finished, he said "That was a very accurate description. I was in that bunker." I was shocked to meet one of the guys who was actually there!

The relationship between Army commanders and their ALO is always a shaky one. The Army commanders never trust the AF since bad weather can keep us away when they need us the most. Today, that problem has been helped a lot by using GPS guided weapons. The pilot no longer has to see the target.

The main irritation the commanders have is that the ALO is not in the Army chain of command. Our relationship with 2AD with this CoS was the best I ever saw, since it was based upon mutual respect, not Service rivalry.

Shortly after our meeting, the division was having its monthly Officers Call with all the division officers (about 200) gathered in the ball room at the Officers Club. The Division Commander introduced the new CoS. The CoS introduced himself and talked about his background. Then he said, "Our only mission is to stop the armored forces of the Warsaw Pact from overrunning Europe. I want every man in this room who has killed an enemy tank in combat to stand up."

The CoS was standing to my left, so I stood up next to him. We were the only two in the room standing. He destroyed two tanks at An

Loc with Light Anti-tank Weapon (LAW) missiles, and I destroyed one with a bomb. He then said, "When this ALO talks about using air strikes against tanks, you listen to him!"

For my last two years there, I was invited to a lot more planning meetings than ever before.

Firepower Demo for Soviet Chiefs of Staff.

As the Cold War seemed to be calming down, the catchword was "Perestroika." That meant a restructuring of the Soviet Union Communist system that supposedly would allow more freedom and aid prosperity. While Brezhnev was leading the USSR, an exchange was arranged between the top military staffs of each country. When the Soviet staff was scheduled to visit the US, they were to visit the top base for each Service.

The Air Force took them to Langley AFB, Tactical Air Command Headquarters and home of the 1st Tactical Fighter Wing, which always got the latest fighters first, the F-15 at that time.

The Navy took them to Norfolk where most of our aircraft carriers are based.

Of course, the Army took them to Fort Hood where all new equipment was deployed first. It was also the largest Army Post.

The 3rd Corps commander was told to provide an impressive firepower demonstration. He was given a million dollars and told that if more was needed, just ask.

I happened to be with the armored brigade considered the best in the Army at the time, so we were tasked to do the demo.

We set up an attack on a defended area. It would open with 6 F-16s dropping two 2,000-pound bombs each on old armored vehicles a mile in front of the attack. An engineer unit would use Bangalore torpedoes (long tubes filled with explosives) and their armored vehicle to breach wire and mine obstacles. Then, M-1 tanks would attack, firing at hard targets and moving pop-up silhouette targets. M-2 armored personnel carriers would follow, unloading their infantry, and providing supporting fire with their 25mm Bushmaster cannons.

Six A-10s would strafe the targets with their 30mm cannons while the infantry was moving forward. All this time, 16 155mm artillery guns would be firing between fighter passes. We even had a radio-controlled model that looked like a Soviet Flogger fighter for our Army Vulcan AAA gunners to shoot. Several old APCs and trucks were set up as targets. Each one had half of a barrel inside that was filled with gasoline to get realistic explosions.

The US Chairman of the Joint Chiefs, Admiral Crowe, was there with his Soviet counterpart. All that firepower concentrated in that small area was devastating. We ruined all the pop-up targets and left an array of burning vehicles throughout the battlefield. When it was over, the Army had one of each of their vehicles that had just participated form a circle with each crew standing in front of their vehicle.

The Soviet delegation (all spoke English) was led into the circle and told they could talk to the troops and look at the vehicles.

We didn't realize at first that the Soviets thought we would have a special group of experts man those vehicles and talk to them. That's the way they would do it. So, when the Soviets went into the circle, they didn't stop. They walked right on through to the other vehicles that were just preparing to leave the demo and talked to those troops, who were completely surprised. Our Army enlisted and junior officers found themselves chatting with the top Soviet military leaders.

ADM Crowe debriefed us later. He said that the Soviets were surprised and impressed by two things.

First, they were amazed when the A-10's appeared just over the treetops firing and hitting all their targets. They appeared and were gone before anyone could react even on repeated passes. The Soviets had not taken the A-10 seriously due to its low speed.

A-10 Firing an EO Guided Maverick

What impressed them by far the most was the Army soldiers. They had always been taught that US soldiers were overweight, out of shape, uneducated, incompetent, nearly all black, and not happy to be there.

They found the opposite. At all three bases, the Soviets found that the US forces were far better than they had thought. I personally

171

believe that this and other demonstrations helped keep us out of conflict with the Russians for several years.

Firepower Demo for news media.

The Army's new APC, the M2 Bradley, was being severely criticized by the news media. It replaced the old M113 APC, which entered service in 1960 and had aluminum armor that was not able to withstand current weapons fire in the 1980s.

The M2 carries a squad of six infantrymen. It was designed with a turret-mounted 25mm gun that can fire 200 armor-penetrating explosive rounds per minute very accurately. The gun is to provide fire support for the infantry that it carries.

Since it is tracked and has a turret, the news media fools insist on calling it a tank. Then, an Air Force colonel in the Pentagon insisted on testing the M2's ability to withstand being hit by an anti-tank missile. It's not a tank, so it wasn't designed to fight tanks or anti-tank weapons.

The test destroyed the M2. That raised outrage among the news media fools that our new "tank" couldn't withstand an anti-tank round.

The Army decided to hold a demonstration for the news networks. It was to show how the M2 was to be used. Also, the news people would get to drive an M2 and an M1 and fire their weapons to show the difference between a tank and an APC. I arranged for a pair of A-10's to show how they support the mission.

We set up a standard attack where the M1's lead the attack. When the tanks have taken initial control of the front, the M2's move in and their infantry troops continue the attack with the M1's and M2's providing fire support. The A-10's would make passes supporting all stages of the attack.

No weapons were actually fired during this entire demonstration attack. All weapons firing was on the live-fire range with the news people doing the shooting. CBS, ABC, NBC, and CNN (all four news networks at that time) all participated. The cost was over a million dollars.

At the end, they all admitted that they had not understood how these vehicles were to be used and that the Bradley was NOT a tank.

The demo was on Friday, January 24, 1986. The networks said that the story would be broadcast Wednesday, the 29th. We were ecstatic that we had stopped the public from being told the negative stories about the Bradley.

Jan 28, the space shuttle Challenger blew up. Our demonstration was never aired by any news network.

Hummer Conversion

I was Vehicle Control Officer for the AF detachment with 2AD. Our jeeps were totally inadequate as I explained earlier. The Army had just started buying High Mobility Multi-purpose Wheeled Vehicles (HMMWV) to replace their jeeps. At that time, we all called them the Hum-Vee. The term "Hummer" started being used a few years later, mainly for the civilian version at first.

The AF decided to buy Hummers for the Tactical Air Control Parties. The first AF Hummers arrived while I was at Ft Hood. I received a message from TAC directing my Vehicle Control NCO and myself to read the manual, teach ourselves all we could about driving them, sign off each other's driver's licenses, then teach everyone else in the detachment.

This put me into the position of "Demo Driver" for a constant stream of VIP visitors who wanted to ride in and even drive this amazing new vehicle. Senior Army officers and NCO's were keenly interested, because their units would start receiving their Hummers soon. Politicians from local, state, and national levels started showing up.

While doing my "self-teaching", I anticipated this and scouted out an area that could show all the Hummer capabilities. It had the 60-degree slope to climb and descend, the 45-degree side slope, the 24-inch vertical step, huge rocks to roll over, a trail with a deep rut to hit at high speed, etc. All of these were impossible with a jeep and most other off-road vehicles.

One of my demos was for the 12AF Operations Officer, a senior colonel who was responsible for the TACPs in 12AF. I showed him my demo route and noticed that he was greatly enjoying it. At the end of the demo, I always asked if they would like to drive. Most accepted the offer immediately unless they had a meeting that would conflict. This colonel practically jumped over to the driver's seat with a huge smile.

He drove it the same route that I took, but faster. He then tried routes that I hadn't tested and made a dent in the bottom of the right door frame. I knew that he had a meeting with senior Army officers after the demo, but I couldn't get him to stop driving until he was ten minutes late.

Later, I found out that he had a modified off-road vehicle at home and spent his weekends 4-wheeling at various locations. I've never seen a colonel so happy to be late for a meeting with generals.

All-Service Basketball Championship Game

This was a very emotional event for me while at Fort Hood.

Each Service has sports teams of various types. All have a basketball team. Each year, there is an All-Service tournament in each sport.

One of my years at Fort Hood, the championship basketball game was Air Force vs Army. The game was played at Fort Hood in the fieldhouse.

There are bleachers on both sides of the court that seat probably 600 on each side. Nearly all of the 40 or so Air Force personnel stationed there attended the game. Of course, there were several hundred Army spectators, too. All of the Army spectators dressed in the Battle Dress Uniform (camouflage) that was standard at that time.

All of the Air Force spectators wore the summer short sleeve blue uniforms to make sure that our team could see us. We sat as a group on the center of the side behind the teams.

It was the most exciting game I have ever seen. Both teams were very good. Neither team led by more than two points the entire game with the lead changing constantly. I can't remember the final score, but the Air Force team took the lead with only a few seconds left and won!

We all went crazy! The official photographer had the team form up at center court for a photo with the trophy in front of them.

Then, the team started yelling for all the blue shirts to join them in the photo. They refused to pose for the photo until all of us were formed up behind them.

Defense from Air Attack Training

I was controlling two A-7s as OPFOR air against a battalion from my brigade during a week of field maneuvering. The A-7s had arrived and were circling the Fort Hood maneuver area.

The M1 tanks and M2 APCs had tucked into a tree line along the north side of a large clearing. They picked large trees and thick bushes to hide under and put some foliage on top of the vehicles.

I was standing next to the battalion commander off to the side of the area. We knew where the vehicles were, but couldn't see them. I told the pilots where their "targets" were, but they couldn't see them either. I had the radio speaker on so that the commander could listen to the action. He was smiling since his troops had hidden so well.

Then, I told the A-7 flight to make a low pass over the clearing parallel to the tree line. They came through at about 500 feet at close to 500 knots.

Instantly, there were smoke clouds from engine starts at each vehicle as they all decided they needed a better hiding position and started moving.

The A-7 pilots got excited and started saying "Tally Ho. I see tanks." "There are three. No. Five!" The other pilot yelled "I see eight tanks and two Bradleys!"

I said "Those are your targets, cleared dry."

As the aircraft made multiple passes simulating bombing the tanks, the battalion commander just stood there, looking straight down, and shaking his head.

I suggested that I give a briefing on reactions to air attack during the formal exercise debriefing. The commander emphatically agreed.

Departure Crash #21

Shortly before I left Fort Hood, I one of two ALOs controlling a 2-ship flight of Air National Guard A-7's as opposition CAS during a field exercise on the west portion of the huge Fort Hood exercise area.

They didn't have any ordnance, so we were having them make realistic weapons delivery passes on our troops. Our guys were supposed to hide as well as they could.

The other ALO had the leader make a north to south run at about 2,000' altitude. I turned to look for the other A-7 when Lead made a quick call: *"Engine Seized!"*. He was still in a 10-degree dive, but the engine seizure stopped the hydraulics and froze the flight controls. Without another radio call, he ejected.

The A-7 passed over all the troops on the ground and crashed into the woods. The pilot had a good chute and landed in an open clearing right in front of the vehicles he had targeted. They were the first people to get to him and found him uninjured.

Hurlburt Field, FL

February 1989

W hile at Fort Hood, I was involved in developing the use of an Airspace Coordination Area (ACA), a new procedure to coordinate CAS with Artillery by turning on and off areas where arty would not fire. We also developed ways to control CAS using new tactics allowed by new stand-off weapons including GPS-guided weapons. This rewrite of the CAS manual led to my next assignment.

Air Ground Operations School (AGOS)

My last three years in the Air Force were at AGOS at Hurlburt Field, FL, as an instructor in the Joint Firepower Control Course (JFCC). This is the same place and course that taught me to be a FAC when I was heading for my O-2 assignment.

I spent the first year as an academic instructor and Chief FAC field instructor and the last two years as the JFCC Course Manager and Chief Field Instructor.

All three years, I was also an instructor in the Battle Staff Course. That course was for senior leaders going to assignments at various combat operations centers.

The AGOS building was an old hangar built for Bomarc anti-aircraft missiles in the 1950's. It was an all sheet-metal exterior with wood frame rooms built into it. It rattled and swayed in thunderstorms and clearly couldn't stand much more.

Trauma for Dawn

The girls had to start new schools as the new school year started shortly after our arrival. We lived in a house we rented on the Rocky Bayou Golf Course in Niceville, FL.

Dawn was in third grade and had to ride a bus to school for the first time. The first day, Barbara took her to the bus stop two houses away. Dawn was a bit nervous about it. She got into the bus and it headed out and around the corner onto the main road.

Barbara decided to follow the bus in case Dawn was upset when they got to school. She got into the car and headed out to follow the bus. By the time she caught up with the bus, it had completed picking up students and was heading toward the school.

Barbara was shocked to see the bus stopped a block ahead of her with smoke pouring from under the hood and the kids bailing out the rear emergency door!

As Barbara stopped, the last of the kids got out, and the driver put out the fire. Neither Barbara nor Dawn wanted to wait for a replacement bus, so Barbara took Dawn on to school. This almost counts as another arrival crash.

Trauma for Gwen

Hurlburt Field had a nice golf course called Gator Lakes. Of course, it had several lakes, some with resident alligators. I joined the golf club right away. It was a great deal. The cost was $100 per year. For that you got unlimited free golf including a cart at Gator Lakes and any other base golf course within 50 miles. That included courses at Eglin AFB, Tyndal AFB, and NAS Pensacola.

On hole number three, you had to hit your second or third shot across a lake to get to the green. There was a 7-foot alligator that lived in the lake. He was named Charlie. He often could be seen laying anywhere around the lake, so it was wise to watch for him. I once walked just three feet past his nose before I saw him. He just ignored me as he did almost all golfers.

Another hole had a 12-foot gator that liked to sun itself on the green. Sometimes you had to just forget a ball that was too close to it and drop another ball the other side of the green. Also, his claws tore big slots in the green every day.

I was teaching Gwen to play golf, so we went to Gator Lakes. On number three, Gwen couldn't yet hit across the lake, so she had to play along a narrow strip of grass left of the lake. One of these times, her ball rolled into a couple of inches of water less than a foot into the lake. Charlie was on the shore the other side of the lake about 100 yards away.

While I walked to my ball, Gwen drove the cart to some grass about 10 yards from her ball. She walked over, reached into the lake, and picked up her ball. As soon as her hand touched the water, Charlie stood up, ran to the lake, and started swimming fast toward Gwen. Gwen ran back to the cart, but Charlie kept coming. As he came ashore right where her ball had been, I yelled for her to drive away.

She did, and Charlie chased the cart for about 50 yards before he decided he couldn't catch it. Then, he went back and swam slowly back across the lake. We didn't think it was wise to stay and finish that hole, so we went on to the next one.

DESERT SHIELD

During my second year at AGOS things got wild. Iraq occupied Kuwait, and the US kicked off Operation DESERT SHIELD. This involved moving large forces to and near Saudi Arabia as Saddam Hussein was ordered to withdraw from Kuwait. Barbara volunteered to be activated by the AF Reserves to work at her augmentee position in Washington, DC.

This left me alone with one daughter in elementary school and the other in middle school. DESERT SHIELD lasted for three months. Then, the operation became DESERT STORM, and the reserves were recalled to active duty, so Barbara was in for the duration. That ended up being an additional four months.

As Christmas arrived, the girls and I drove to Arlington, VA, to stay with her for a couple of days. That turned out to be the last trip ever made by our 1983 BMW 528e, which we bought while stationed in England.

Home Disasters While Barbara Was Gone

Everything started to go wrong while Barbara was fighting the war. When I returned to Florida, the refrigerator died. I had to buy a new one without Barbara's input. Then, the washer died, so I had to get a new washer.

A few weeks later, I scheduled both girls to get dental checkups on the same day at the end of the school day. I left work in time to pick them up.

On the way, I was on a 45-mph divided road through Niceville. A lady doctor leaving the hospital in a Volvo failed to see me since her view was blocked by another car, and pulled out right in front of me.

I left three feet of skid marks (no antiskid in those days) before hitting her Volvo directly in the driver's door. I got a minor whiplash from being stopped by the shoulder harness. She got a bump on her head from hitting the left side window. Both cars were totaled. That was the end of our BMW 528e. We had 141,000 miles on it over eight years with many of those in Europe. I really enjoyed cruising at 120mph on the Autobahn.

Barbara had to take leave and drive our other car back to Florida so we could jointly buy a new car. I presented Barbara with half of the plate we had on the front license bracket. The plate was black plastic with "HERS" in large gold letters. I found it embedded in the Volvo driver's door. Then, we bought our first of three consecutive Mercury Sables.

AGOS Goes to War

Next, the AF sent half of my AGOS instructors to Saudi Arabia to teach joint firepower control to Arab Corps FACs, of which there were none at that time. Luckily, I could take over teaching any course in AGOS and most in the Battle Staff Course. Most of the few instructors left could also pick up extra courses. In Saudi Arabia, the idea was to spend a few weeks training Arab FACs to control CAS and then return to Hurlburt where we were increasing the size of the AGOS classes.

The Arab countries had never really done CAS. Each Sheik had his own piece of the military. It might be an armored battalion, an artillery battalion, a fighter squadron, etc. The King never allowed the various pieces to practice working together for fear of a coup. Thus, there was no concept of coordination or mutual support between air and ground forces or even different types of ground forces.

The AF asked for FAC students who were familiar with watching and/or controlling fighters and spoke English. Something important was left out. They knew nothing at all about fighter weapons or tactics. They straggled into the room for class hours late and were all civilian air traffic controllers.

In the US, most FACs are prior fighter pilots. In fact, that was mandatory for a long time. We asked the Saudi's to send us a few fighter pilots. Arab fighter pilots are pretty much all sons of sheiks or rich businessmen. There is no way that any of them would agree to go on the ground with the army as an ALO.

The few poorly qualified men sent to train never showed up on time for class. 10AM to them meant any time midday. When our instructors scheduled aircraft for them to control, the planes would come and leave before any trainees would show up.

As the start of combat (DESERT STORM) approached, no Arab FACs were successfully trained. This resulted in a decision to keep the AGOS instructors there, and send them into the field with the Arab Corps. Of course, there were TACPs deploying with each of the numerous US Army units. A few extra TACP Hummers and Tactical Air Control Specialists (the new name for the enlisted member of a TACP) were sent to join up with my AGOS instructors who were now ALOs with the Arabs.

I started receiving letters from Battalion ALOs who were already deployed. Most of them were A-10 pilots with a few F-16 pilots. In fact, I had trained every American ALO and FAC that deployed. Some of the letters had a lot of fine dust in them. One even said he was writing from a foxhole! Everyone thanked me for my class on living in field conditions with the Army.

They mostly said that they needed everything they learned about integrating air into the ground battle, but that my warnings about how bad it would be in the field with the Army weren't strong enough. At AGOS, they didn't believe me about how bad the Army would treat them, but now they said it should have been stressed more.

The fact is that most Army Battalion Commanders looked at the ALO as an extra junior officer who could be used for any task. They refused to admit that the ALO is not in their chain of command. I have seen a 2LT ALO be ordered to be in charge of night perimeter security of the Tactical Operations Center. Why would a commander want someone with no training at all in ground combat to handle his TOC security?

By this time, all airborne FACs were either Air Force pilots flying the OA-10 or Navy pilots flying the F-14. An OA-10 is an A-10 with an FM radio added to talk to the Army. ALOs and airborne FACs no longer swapped positions. Each was with his unit for the duration.

There were many heroic acts by ALOs, especially those with the Arab units leading the attack into Kuwait. All returned unharmed. I received several great after-action reports from both ALOs and FACs that were useful in refining tactics and procedures. You may have heard about a couple of fratricide incidents where friendlies were killed by air attack. Both of them were non-certified US Army or British Army members controlling aircraft even though they were not trained for that.

AGOS Computers

There was no computer network in our building. We had ten old computers with 9-inch green screens and a 5 ¼ inch floppy drive. These were used only for class reviews by students and a Condor database for class registration. I wrote the database application for this. It was my first program for actual use by others.

For instructors and admin, we had six Zenith Z-100 computers with color monitors, 10-megabyte hard drive, and 5 ¼ inch floppy drive. All of our lesson plans and texts were on the hard drives on the

Z-100's. They were backed up on floppies that were kept on top of the computers.

As the default computer guru, I started insisting that we needed off-site backup. The old hangar that AGOS was in was the closest building to the beach and was not safe in a storm. It took me two years and a new commandant to get anyone to agree to that.

During that time, I made copies of the floppy disk backups and put them in a metal filing cabinet. Finally, shortly before I retired and left, we started keeping backup copies of the floppies in a vault at the Special Operations Wing intelligence center at Hurlburt.

Departure Crash #22

There was always a crash when I left an assignment, but leaving for retirement was a much bigger event. A year after I left, a hurricane hit Hurlburt directly, completely destroying the AGOS building. This is the second building where I had worked destroyed by a non-combat disaster.

The Air Force decided not to rebuild at Hurlburt and moved the AGOS to Nellis AFB, Las Vegas, NV. The good news was that the school information was backed up and in the Special Operations Wing vault nice and dry.

Nellis was probably the only other suitable place that had areas nearby to train ground operations, controlling artillery, and controlling air support. What a crazy move; tropical climate to desert. Tough on families. We were really glad that we left before that happened.

I suppose that after 11 arrival crashes, 22 departure crashes, and 2 destroyed hangars, it was good for the Air Force that I left. I'm not taking credit for the entire destroyed base in the Philippines. Of course, I was only directly involved in one. For the era of the F-100 through the F-111, this was about normal. The amazing part of this is that no squadron I was in suffered a major accident or a combat loss while I was actively flying with them, with the huge exception of mine at Kunsan.

Retirement

I retired with 20 years of active duty 29 February 1992. Barbara continued for a total of 27 years combined active duty and reserve duty before retiring. Then, we both worked for Department of Defense agencies for another 20 years and retired from Civil Service. Both of us made good use of the skills and knowledge we learned in the Air Force while in civilian service. We have spent nearly our entire adult lives dedicated to the defense of our country.

I now volunteer at the Smithsonian Udvar-Hazy Center at Washington Dulles Airport. I teach how a plane is controlled including having them sit in a Cessna 206 and operate the controls. It's fun and fulfilling, because during my 3-hour shift as many as 150 excited children, including entire elementary school classes, come to that display.

Many adults also enjoy it. Nearly all have been in an airliner, but very few know what happens in the cockpit. It's the only aircraft in the museum that allows visitors to climb in and move the controls, so it's usually the kid's favorite.

I am also an instructor at the Space Shuttle cockpit simulator. It's a handful to land due to sloppy aerodynamic controls and high landing speed. In fact, it lands at a little over 200 knots, just like the F-105G. The challenge of landing a Thud safely was actually good training on how to land a Space Shuttle.

I particularly enjoy spending a few hours there each week, because I feel a strong connection to the displays. There is an F-4B and an F-105D that I can see from the Cessna. I have counted seven aircraft there that I have actually seen fly. One of them is Burt Rutan's prototype Varieze, which inspired Barbara and I to build one.

I have been an Experimental Aircraft Association member since 1974. I joined EAA chapter 186 at Manassas, Virginia, recently. I don't maintain flying currency any more, but I assist at events including airshows. Manassas Airport is where the large historic aircraft stage for ceremonial flybys over Washington, DC.

Also, there is a Young Eagles rally once each month where chapter members take young people aged 7-17 and interested in becoming a pilot for 20-minute flights. I assist in that operation.

Barbara has published three children's books with more in the works. As we keep busy during retirement, we hope and pray that many other young Americans chose to spend their lives dedicated to defense.

Found Our Varieze

Do you remember that when we moved to England, we had to sell the Varieze that we had nearly completed building? While writing this in May 2020, *I found it.* The guy I sold it to never did any more work on it. A year after he bought it, he sold it to a guy who intended to finish it quickly. In fact, that guy had looked at it at my house a year earlier. He decided not to buy it at that time. When he discovered that it was for sale again, he immediately drove a truck to the owner and bought it.

The second buyer had several circumstances that kept him from getting to it for 15 years. By the time he got to it, Burt Rutan had made several improvements to the plans, so he added those to my work as he finished it. That took him a year. He bought a used engine for it from Dick Rutan, Burt's brother.

This owner flew it for several years around the northwest part of the US. In 2013, he sold it to a man in Vancouver, Canada, who still flies it. The photo of the yellow aircraft on the cover of this book is that Varieze.

Someday, we hope to get to Vancouver and get a ride in it.

Glossary

1Lt	First Lieutenant	Second Lowest AF officer rank
2Lt	Second Lieutenant	Lowest AF officer rank
A1C	Airman First Class	Highest AF rank below Sergeant
AAA	Anti-Aircraft Artillery	Guns to defend against aircraft
AB	Air Base	A base not owned by the USAF
AFB	Air Force Base	An air base owned by the USAF
AGOS	Air/Ground Operations School	Teaches coordination of air power with ground maneuver
ALO	Air Liaison Officer	Air Force pilot on the ground with an Army unit who coordinates with ground forces and controls air support
ANG	Air National Guard	
Arty	Artillery	Guns of various sizes that fire from a distance without directly aiming at a target
IP	Instructor Pilot or Initial Point	An Initial Point is the last navigation reference point before a target
Bingo	Go-home Fuel State	Fuel amount to safely return to base
CAS	Close Air Support	Air attacks on targets close enough to friendlies that they require very close coordination with the ground force
Disco	Call sign for the EC-121 radar aircraft	Today's equivalent is the Air Warning and Control System (AWACS)
DMZ	Demilitarized Zone	Zone separating North and South Vietnam established to keep peace. Failed miserably.
EWO	Electronic Warfare Officer	Operates all electronic warfare equipment on the aircraft including radar jammers and

		radar warning systems. Also functions as WSO during weapons delivery.
FAC	Forward Air Controller	Air Force pilot, either airborne or on the ground, who coordinates with ground forces and controls Close Air Support. Some non-pilots are certified as Emergency FACs
Fingertip Formation		4 aircraft positioned like the fingertips of a hand held flat
FM	Frequency Modulated	Radio type used mostly by Army
G	One time the force of gravity	Twice gravity = 2Gs, Three times = 3Gs, etc.
GCA	Ground Controlled Approach	A GCA controller sits in a trailer next to a radar trailer next to the center of the runway and talks the pilots down through bad weather.
GCI	Ground Controller Intercept	A controller at a radar site who vectors interceptors to targets they cannot see on their own radar.
GPS	Global Positioning System	Satellites that provide very accurate position on Earth plus a very precise timing signal
INS	Inertial Navigation System	Keeps track of aircraft location based on movement
Interdiction	Interdiction Mission	Attacking targets in the enemy rear area not near friendly forces
IP	Instructor Pilot	A pilot with special training to teach others to fly an aircraft
Knots	Nautical Miles Per Hour	About 1.15 times US standard miles per hour Examples: 200 knots = 230 mph and 600 knots = 690 mph
LPU	Life Preserver Unit	Attached to survival vest in arm

		pits. Inflates to provide flotation.
Mach	Speed of sound	Mach 1 = 761 knots or 661 miles per hour. Mach 2 = twice the speed of sound, etc.
MCAS	Marine Corps Air Station	
MK-82	500 lb General Purpose Bomb	Used as the basis for several versions using precision guided seeker heads with control fins
NAS	Naval Air Station	
NATOPS	Naval Air Training and Operating Procedures Standardization	All Navy weapons systems have a NATOPS manual that states how to use them.
NCO	Non-commissioned Officer	All enlisted ranks above A1C
NM	Nautical Mile	About 1.15 standard miles
NVN	North Vietnam	See Map
REFORGER	Redeployment of Forces To Germany	An exercise to practice moving US forces back to Germany if the post WWII peace does not hold.
ROTC	Reserve Officer Training Corps	
RP	Route Pack	NVN was divided into 6 route packs
SAM	Surface to Air Missile	In Vietnam, usually an SA-2 radar guided missile or an SA-7 heat seeker.
SAR	Search and Rescue	Rescue helicopters defended by highly maneuverable fighters with various weapons
SVN	South Vietnam	See Map at end
TAC	Tactical Air Command	Commanded all TFWs in the Continental US
TACAN	Tactical Air Navigation system	A ground based system that radiates signals in all directions. Signals are coded to tell

		direction to TACAN and distance from it in NM
TACCS	Tactical Air Command and Control Specialist	Enlisted member of TACP. Expert with comm systems and trained as Emergency FAC
TACP	Tactical Air Control Party	ALO, TACCS, & their vehicle & radios located with Army units
TFW	Tactical Fighter Wing	Usually 4 squadrons
TFS	Tactical Fighter Squadron	Usually 18-24 fighter aircraft
UPT	Undergraduate Pilot Training	Initial pilot training. After getting your wings here, you attend training for a specific aircraft.
WP	White Phosphorus	Usually Willie Pete. Warhead breaks open at impact and burns on contact with air, making a small cloud of bright white smoke.
WSO	Weapons System Operator	Handles radar and electronic countermeasures in F-4, F-111, and a few other aircraft.

A Request From the Author

Thank you for reading my story. I hope that you found it interesting, informative, and, at times, exciting.

If you enjoyed reading it, I would appreciate hearing from you by your writing a review on Amazon at:
https://www.amazon.com/dp/B08D7WMCKG

I greatly appreciate your support and hope you share this story with others of similar interests. This could be important reading for anyone considering a military career. It might also help understand a loved one who returns from combat or other dangerous situations a somewhat different person.

About the Author

Chuck Banks was born in northern Indiana two years after WWII ended. It was a period of recovery from the two World Wars and then the Korean War. The Cold War followed. He experienced the fear and anxiety of growing up in a world where unstoppable nuclear missiles were only 30 minutes away at all times and world leaders were constantly threatening each other. Russia's Nikita Khrushchev even emphasized his threats by pounding on the table at the United Nations with his shoe, and exclaimed "We will bury you!" He may have meant economically, but it seemed to be a dual meaning.

Chuck developed a deep need to help protect his country and its people from the terrors of Communist giants and religious terrorists bent on world domination. He completed his education and became a fighter pilot in time to participate in the last year of the Vietnam war. The rest of his career was spent training and preparing for the possibility of even bigger wars, hoping that our preparedness would deter the start of one.

After 20 years, he retired from the Air Force, and continued participating in defending the US while working in various Department of Defense agencies for a second 20-year career.

Made in the USA
Coppell, TX
23 November 2022

86913268R00115